KEEP IT
SHORT

A Practical
Guide to
Writing in
the 21st
Century

"Charlie Euchner tells writers to keep it simple, then shows them how. The process of creating great writing couldn't be explained any better...or simpler."
– **J.M. DeBord, author of *Dreams 1 2 3*, *Big Book of Dream Interpretation*, and Dream Moderator, Reddit.com**

Published by Lisa Hagan Books 2016

Powered by

SHADOW TEAMS

Copyright © Charles Euchner

ISBN: 9780976498681

Cover design and interior layout by Simon Hartshorne

CHARLES EUCHNER

KEEP IT
SHORT

A Practical
Guide to
Writing in
the 21st
Century

The pages crackle and vibrate with the voices of unsung heroes who drove, flew, rode buses and trains, hitchhiked, even walked long distances to be there in the Great Emancipator's stone shadow as Dr. King spun out his immortal 'Dream.'"

    — John Egerton, author, *Speak Now Against the Day: The Generation Before the Civil Rights Movement in the South*

The Last Nine Innings*:*
The Last Nine Innings is the last word on the inside game of baseball. It's full of wonderful revelations and perceptions that help us understand the game in ways that we might never have imagined. Charlie Euchner has done a marvelous job in getting players to talk, simply, about how they play, and we're the wiser for it."

    — Frank Deford, National Public Radio, HBO "Real Sports," and *Sports Illustrated*

Rip out the red thread on the baseball, peel back the cowhide, and talk about the stuff that's wound up inside the game. That's what Charles Euchner does in *The Last Nine Innings*, and it's fascinating."

    — Leigh Montville, author of *Ted Williams: A Biography*

Playing the Field*:* This landmark work should anger taxpayers and inspire them to stand up to the millionaires pulling the strings behind teams and governments, entities citizens still naively consider their own."

    — Eliot Cohen, *Cooperstown Review*

Urban Policy Reconsidered (with Stephen McGovern): For those of us who believe that American cities have a bright future ahead of them, this is a timely, thoughtful and invaluable road map to that future. You may or may not agree with all of their policy prescriptions, but if you care about our urban communities, this is a must read book."

    — Michael Dukakis, former governor of Massachusetts and 1988 Democratic presidential nominee

Contents

I have made this longer than usual because
I have not had time to make it shorter.

—Blaise Pascal

What's the problem?

....

#**THE PROBLEM**

....

> *Everyone says to keep it short,*
> *but few succeed. Here's why.*

Sometimes you ask a simple question and you get a Zen koan.

As an aspiring journalist, just a kid, I sometimes wrote to my favorite writers seeking advice. One of those writers was Robert Creamer, the longtime writer for *Sports Illustrated* and the author of *Babe,* which remains the seminal biography of Babe Ruth more than forty years after its publication. What, I asked, could I do to become a good writer? Creamer responded with a one-sentence letter—not even using his own words.

"Brevity is the soul of wit," he said, quoting Shakespeare.

Easier noted than achieved, Mr. Creamer.

Writers start out with good intentions. More often than not, though, we get tangled in long, meandering sentences that lost sight of their goal. Once we sit down to write, by longhand or on a keyboard, the words skitter out like commuters emerging from a New York subway station—bumping and jostling, some going this way and others that way, weaving, halting and backtracking, and ultimately spinning into too many destinations to manage.

What happens?

Two things—creativity and confusion.

Let's start with creativity. When we write, we rev up the engine of our minds to explore ideas that often zoom off whether we mean it or not. Our minds are *associative engines*, as the brain scientists tell us. When we think a particular thought, that thought prompts us to think other thoughts. Let me show you. Tell me what you think about when I prompt you with the word *beach.*

That word prompted me to think of the words *sun, saltwater, surf, suntan,* and *waves.*

Now, let me ask you to name a laundry detergent.

Did you do as I expected? Did you say *Tide*?

Prompted by beach-related words, almost everyone says *Tide.* Tide is an established, venerable brand, with a market share of about 40 percent of laundry detergent sales. But almost *everyone* says Tide when prompted with these seaside terms.

The same thing happens when you write. As you write, you explore a wide range of ideas. Each one prompts a chain of associations. Often those associations prompt complete thoughts. Those new thoughts usually have *something* to do with the subject of your writing. But often, they veer away from that subject. Once you veer away, you often forget what you were writing about in the first place.

Let me give you an example. Suppose you are writing about the pervasive influence of celebrities in modern America. You might start with something like this:

> Celebrity in America has always given us an outlet for our imagination, just as the gods and demigods of ancient Greece and Rome once did.

Good start. What now? Well, you might think of specific celebrities that "offer an outlet for our imagination"—Adele or Madonna, Tom Brady or Giselle Bunchen, Jay Z or Donald Trump. And, right then and there, you might want to talk about them. So you might continue like this:

> Donald Trump illustrates the power of celebrity, and in fact he dominated the 2016 presidential campaign despite his lack of experience in government.

Not bad, but note that we might be veering off course. If we forget the premise of the opening sentence, we might proceed like this:

> Trump, in fact, displayed real ignorance about basic public policy issues. He vowed to torture war combatants, in violation of American and international law. He could not explain the concept of "nuclear triad,"

the most basic concept of American military policy. And he blamed the Chinese for a trade agreement that did not involve the Chinese.

Sentence by sentence, we spin away from the original topic—celebrity as an outlet for the imagination.

One idea prompts another, which prompts another, which prompts another. On one level, that's great. Writing is a process of discovery. When you sit down to write, all kinds of great ideas pour out—some of which you had no idea you'd explore when you sat down to write. Great writers often say that they have little control over where their stories go. William Faulkner put it this way:

> It begins with a character, usually, and once
> he stands up on his feet and begins to move,
> all I can do is trot along behind him with
> a paper and pencil trying to keep up long
> enough to put down what he says and does.

Faulkner was talking about storytelling, but the same thing happens with all kinds of writing—academic analyses, company memos, consulting reports, descriptions and explanations. We can paraphrase Faulkner like this:

> It begins with an idea, usually, and once I
> express that idea, all I can do is follow that

idea, with a paper and pencil, trying to keep up long enough to put down where it leads me.

Creativity is a wild animal, full of energy and life but hard to control. To control this beast, we need to know where we want to take it. We cannot get distracted or sidetracked.

But creativity is just half of the problem. The other half is confusion. Think back to what I said a moment ago: *Writing is a process of discovery.* Often, when we start to write something, we don't know all we need to know. We sit down to scribble or type before we have done adequate research. Maybe we were lazy. Or we thought we knew what we needed to explain a topic. So what happens? All too often, we try to write without enough information or insight. Confident that ideas will "come to me," we press forward and try to bull our way through sentences and paragraphs.

That's when things get ugly. When we try to bull our way through a topic, we commit three deadly sins:

We repeat ourselves.

We use vague phrasing — adjectives and generalizations — instead of clear, crisp details and logic.

We ramble, piling words and phrases, with the hope that we will discover some telling detail or concept—but usually moving further and further away from the point.

Let's see how that happens with the discussion of celebrity. After writing the original sentence about celebrity as an outlet for imagination, we might grope to develop the thought but simply restate the point over and over:

> When we worship celebrities, it's as if we're worshipping gods. We look up to celebrities as if they have magical powers. Celebrities have a unique power to attract our attention—and we seem to think they can do more than they actually can.

Or we use generalizations:

> Celebrities have a lot of power over us. They dazzle us with their beauty and seeming power. They are larger than life as they move from one place to another. They seem bigger and smarter that "ordinary" people and capture our attention with their dazzling smiles and how easily they move around and …

Or we ramble, not sure where we're going:

> Celebrity worship happens in a wide variety of fields, like show business and sports and even politics, which changes the whole way people make decisions about public policy on matters like taxes, health care, foreign policy, and …

In these ways, we lose control of the topic. Who can even remember the clearly stated point of the paragraph?

Now let's see how a pro does the job. Look how Jill Niemark develops her argument about celebrity, imagination, and mythology. In *Psychology Today* in 2010, Niemark writes:

> Celebrity in America has always given us an outlet for our imagination, just as the gods and demigods of ancient Greece and Rome once did. Celebrities are our myth bearers; carriers of the divine forces of good, evil, lust, and redemption. "The wish for kings is an old and familiar wish, as well-known in medieval Europe as in ancient Mesopotamia," writes Lewis Lapham in his book *The Wish For Kings*. ... Once the famous were recorded for the ages in stone and in paint. Alexander the Great was the first famous person in a modern sense, contends Leo Braudy, Ph.D., professor of English at the University of Southern California and author of *The Frenzy of Renown*. "Not only did he want to be unique, but he wanted to tell everybody about it..."

Niemark develops her point about celebrity, adding detail and expert testimony, sentence after sentence. She never gets distracted. She never drives off the road.

And so we come to the core lesson. To write simply

and clearly—to "keep it short"—you need to know what you want to say. You need to avoid the temptation to veer off. Whatever you say, you have to follow up with specific information about that topic.

Brevity is the soul of wit. True enough. But to be brief—to stay clear and concise—you need to know your subject and stay on point. It's not always easy. But with a dozen or so simple tricks, you can do it.

....
#**PURPOSE**
....

Follow the Admiral James Stockdale rule.
Ask: "Who am I and why am I here?"

Why do you want to write? To entertain? Narrate? Inform? Explain? Question? Cajole? Persuade? Convert? Anger?

And who to you wish to address? Friends? Colleagues? Professionals? Experts? Lay people? Locals? Cosmopolitans? Informed or less-informed people? People with inklings or prejudices—people with passions for causes—or not?

Lots of writers don't know what they want to do, or with whom, when they sit down to a keyboard. They imagine a vast world of PLUs—"people like us"—who will follow a piece effortlessly. But it's not that easy. That's why I want you to answer the Admiral Stockdale Question every time to sit down to write—*not just at the beginning of the project, but every single time you sit down to write.*

In 1992, Stockdale was plucked from obscurity to run for vice president with the billionaire Ross Perot. In the first VP debate, he opened with the bracing question: "Who am I and why am I here?"

If you answer this question, you will write better, clearer, zippier, and faster. If you don't, you will meander and wander, repeating yourself and changing the subject. You will confuse yourself and your reader as well.

To understand the importance of purpose, think of the concept of *alignment*.

Ideally, we live our lives in alignment with our values, goals, capabilities, and resources. Do you have a dream job? If so, I bet your daily activities match your personal values. If you value physical activity, fitness, and health, you are (probably) better off running a hiking organization than an accountancy firm. If you value the life of the mind, you're better off working as a researcher or teacher or writer. If you value helping people, you will thrive as a teacher, social worker, doctor or nurse, counselor, or coach.

Fitting your activity with your values is just the beginning. If I want to be a pro baseball player, I had better have superior strength, endurance, hand-eye coordination, a zest for competition, and so on. And I had better devote endless hours to honing my skills.

Likewise, as writers, we need to align our writing with ourselves and our audiences.

So ask yourself: What do you want to achieve as a

writer? Do you want to be a clear, breezy writer? Do you want to tell stories, develop characters, and depict action and scenes? Do you want to explain complex concepts, break them down into simple pieces, and then connect those pieces? Do you want to persuade your audience?

Or maybe you want to engage in intellectual fencing matches. Or interact like a litigator in court. Or empathize, connecting with your audience's values and feelings. Maybe you want to be serious or funny.

Part of the answer comes from who you are. I know academics who construct elaborate abstract arguments, which focus on logic and evidence and eschew humor and intrigue. I know other academics who regale readers with creative approaches to issues, telling stories, cracking jokes, and surprising you with clever twists of logic. It all depends on who you are and what is your purpose.

Essayists show a wide range of personas. Some are homey and engaging (E.B. White, Thomas Lynch) while others are pointed and acerbic (Maureen Dowd, Christopher Hitchens) and still others are cool and detached (Joan Didion). Some speak formally, while others use colloquial, informal banter (David Foster Wallace, Hunter Thompson).

The central issue for deciding your voice, though, is how you want to tell a story or explain and analyze an issue. Consider this quick guide.

Storytelling	Explanation/analysis
Take the reader on a direct journey, beginning at the beginning and ending at the end.	Show, step-by-step, how something works— like a recipe or set of instructions from Ikea.
Create a more dramatic story, with mysteries running from start to finish	Identify a topic to explore, then breaking it up into pieces to explore, one by one.
Move back and forth, using flashbacks when needed to provide background	Making an argument— which comes down to a statement of cause and effect.
In media res: Starting in the "middle," backtracking to get to that start and then proceeding to tell the rest of the story.	Raising questions— without intending to answer them—in order to show the different dimensions of a topic.

To figure out your approach, ask yourself: Just where are your readers as you begin the journey? Where are you? Are you on the cusp of a great narrative journey—or a more logical exploration of a person, place, or idea?

Now that you know your starting point, do you know where you're going?

....
#FRAMING/SCOPE
....

To understand anything, we first focus on the frames—what marks the beginnings and endings. Once we understand the frame, we can focus on the details inside the frame.

What do you want to talk about? I mean, *specifically*, what do you want your readers to ponder?

That's a more difficult question than we sometimes realize.

Every day, we have free-flowing conversations about our families, jobs, politics, faith, sports, relationships, pets, cars, food, clothing—all of the stuff of everyday life. When we talk about these things, we constantly shift our focus. We shuffle between the specific and the general. We toggle between the here-and-now and the past or future. We move back and forth between cold, hard reality and speculation and fantasy. We alternate between certainty and doubt, optimism and pessimism, open and closed mindsets. Consider this conversation:

A: How's the new job?
B: Not bad, considering.

A: Considering what? What have you been doing?

B: They started me out with a weeklong orientation—lectures, drills, bonding exercises. You know the drill.

A: Yeah, everyone's doing that these days. It's their way of making you feel welcome. Or is it their way of mind control?

B: Yeah, mind control. There was this guy who left the place using all the phrases of the instructors: "life's journey," "mission," "plan for success."

A: Any decent people there?

B: A few. I hit it off with a woman from Tennessee. She's just out of school. I thought she was standoffish at first, but everything she said was funny, cracked me up.

A: You going to ask her out?

B: I would … but we're going to be working together. Maybe she'll get transferred to a different department. I don't know.

A: I was once in a situation like that. We started going out, in secret, but it just created all kinds of awkward situations. Those things can't work, at least not usually. No, never. Such a bummer. What's the place where you meet compatible people? Work. But you can't do anything—you can't go out.

B: Well, you never know. Anyway, one of the speakers was the founder of the company. He's 80 now. He still comes to work every day. He has meetings with people working out—lifting weights, walking, running.

A: If you keep fit, you can work forever. Or travel. That's what I want to do. I want to go to all continents. How many are there anyway? Does Antarctica count? Are Europe and Asia separate or are they one mega-continent—Eurasia?

B: You can last forever if you have good genes. My family has good genes. I should eat better, to take advantage of that. My grandfather lived till he was 95. I might make that, if I can get my act together.

A: I'm doomed. All my grandparents died in their 60s.

B: Well, you could exercise more . . .

A: Wouldn't help.

B: Well, I just want to figure out how to advance in this company. I'd like to run the IT department some day. I'd love to work in the L.A. office. Can you imagine? Working in L.A., living in Santa Monica, going out with Hollywood types …

These people are all over the place. They track each others' thoughts reasonably well. Body language and tone of voice do a good job signaling shifts in focus or emphasis.

Most conversations are collections of ideas and feelings, not well-constructed discourses.

But as writers, we need to express ideas—and the context of those ideas—more clearly. We can't rely on body language or tone of voice to convey ideas. We need to organize ideas into clearly demarcated sentences and paragraphs and pieces. We need to know when we are talking about specific or general, here or before or later, realistic or speculative, and so on.

When we write, we need to pick out a single idea to frame our discussion. The conversation above could focus on a number of topics:

- Starting a new job.
- The nature of work in the modern age.
- Romance.
- Office romance.
- Living a good life.
- Health.

One of biggest causes of loggerhea—excessive talking or wordiness—is uncertainty. Rather than grounding the conversion on a clear topic, we shift around. When we shift, we lose track of the context. When we lose track, we double-back and explain where we are. Those explanations can take us off on new tangents.

If you don't frame your discussion well, you will fall into confusion. So you need to decide: *What's the one story or idea I want to explore here, with narrative or explanation? What other ideas can help me to explore that idea? And what ideas cannot?*

Part 1

Narrative and structure

Years ago, TV and radio stations in New York aired commercials for an appliance store open only to union members. The store's owner, Jerry Rosenberg, stars in the commercial. A character offstage prompts him, again and again: "Hey Jerry, what's the story?" After each question, Jerry explains how the store works. If you work for a union or the government, you can get discounts on electronics, appliances, and furniture. In his Brooklyn accent, Jerry calls out: "Just show your union card at the door, and you're in!" Finally, prompted by the character offstage, Jerry calls out: "That's the *stooory!*"

Jerry knew his story: If you work hard for a living and pay your union dues, you are entitled to lower costs on consumer goods. You could depict the story like this:

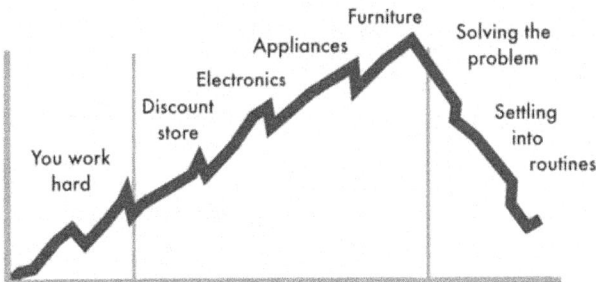

With every question, the benefits increase. Finally, the problem is solved.

Now, I need to ask: What's *your* story?

....
#CHARACTER
....

To give your writing focus, zoom in on a character or idea to engage the reader emotionally and intellectually.

Every great piece of writing shows at least one character who engages the reader's heart and mind.

Think of your favorite characters from books, movies, TV, and gaming: From ancients like Oedipus, Antigone, Odysseus, and the gods of the Greeks and Romans. Or Shakespeare's sprawling cast: Julius Caesar, Prince Hal/King Henry, Hamlet and Lear, Macbeth and his Lady, Violas and Titiana/Hippolyta, Prospero, Falstaff, Iago, and Puck. Think of great characters from novels: Don Quixote, Oblomov, Huck Finn, Catherine and Heathcliff, Anna Karenenna, Jay Gatsby, Scout, Ignatius Reilly, and Lisbeth Salander. On and on the list goes.

To get emotionally involved with a story, the reader needs to *care* about characters. Readers need to invest themselves in the character's development. Characters embody different aspects of the human psyche. They are aggressive and timid, cerebral and emotional, wise and impulsive, friendly and formal.

The leading character does not need to be a person.

Writers have told riveting stories by following a gun (Erik Larson's *Lethal Passage*), an animal (Michael Pollan's *Power Steer*), and insecticides (Rachel Carson's *Silent Spring*), to note just a few.

Alfred Hitchcock used a device he called the McGuffin—an object or an idea that the story's characters want to obtain. The McGuffin has mysterious and powerful qualities. The greatest of all McGuffins is the Holy Grail, a dish or cup with magical powers. Other famous McGuffins include the word "rosebud" (*Citizen Kane*), a statuette of a black bird (*The Maltese Falcon*), letters of transit (*Casablanca*), a Heart of the Ocean necklace (*Titanic*), a ring (*Lord of the Rings*), and a broom (*The Wizard of Oz*). The search for this object or idea—and the struggle involved in the search—gets us emotionally invested in the topic. *We care.*

Let's track how Michael Pollan uses an object as a character. In *The Botany of Desire*, Pollan follows the life of corn to understand the changing politics and economics of agriculture. He traces the greater productivity of corn production (the yield per acre has increased from 20 to 160 in a century) and the countless ways corn has become part our diet and energy supply. To Pollan, corn explains the growth of fast food, the cattle industry, obesity, environmental problems, outbreaks of disease, and government regulation and subsidies. He uses a head of cattle in *Power Steer* to make a similar analysis of the beef industry.

So characters—or character-like objects or ideas—matter. How then do we identify or create them?

I like to use two techniques—the Character Dossier and the Wheel of Archetypes.

....
#**THE DOSSIER**
....

When you write, you need to act like a private investigator. You need to gather facts to discover *what matters* about your subject. Most of what you discover won't matter. But you need to gather the stones to find the diamonds.

The Character Dossier offers a complete questionnaire about a story's character—family, schooling, passions and fears, turning points and moments of truth, friends and foes, and more.

Every story begins with characters. For the story to "go" anywhere, it needs someone we might care about—a character full of complexity and contradictions, with some kind of vision and mission, who sees the world in a distorted way and makes mistakes but is also open to change. Any time I write a story, I start with the dossier. At the end, if I cannot answer all of its questions with immediate, specific, emotional scenes, I know I have not finished my work.

Personal Background

- Name
- Age and birthday
- Birthplace
- Parents' ethnic and religious background, upbringing, hopes and fears, and careers
- Place in the family's birth order
- Relations with siblings and other relatives

Physical Characteristics

- Body Build
- Hair and eye color
- Sound of voice
- Conversational tics
- Physical peculiarities
- Mannerisms while walking, talking, working, and playing

Growing With Others

- Pastimes as a child ... and as an adult
- Sidekicks and mentors
- Intellectual and emotional influences
- Rivals and foes at different stages of life
- Not-so-good influences—skeptics, and tempters
- Political leanings—and major political influences
- What others notice first
- How the character changes over the course of life
- Turning points in life

Psychology

- All-consuming desires
- Pathological maneuver
- Most admirable qualities
- Least admirable qualities
- Sexual identity
- Philosophy of life
- Optimism or pessimism
- Energy level
- What the character does when alone

The best stories provide complete portraits of all the major characters, even some minor ones.

Happily, when you create dossiers for your main characters, you go along way toward telling your story. Your characters take you along for the ride—if you let them.

I use the dossier at my writing seminars to teach character development and storytelling. One of my favorite sessions took place at Hillhouse High School in New Haven, Connecticut. A dozen or so students came to school on a Saturday to develop writing skills. We started with the dossier.

One by one, students offered answers to the dossier questions to create a character. Every answer foreclosed other possibilities—and opened new possibilities. When the first student named the character Jody, we knew we probably had a girl, probably from the U.S. When the next person gave her birthday, we knew she was sixteen. When someone gave her a slender, athletic build, we knew she was vital and alive. Detail by detail, we created a memorable character:

> Jodie is a sixteen-year-old orphan being raised by her grandparents. Slender and athletic, with brown hair and hazel eyes, Jodie still struggles with the trauma of her parents' deaths in a plane crash. She lights candles in her room and holds *séances* to connect with her lost parents; in a bit of "magical thinking," she thinks she can somehow bring them back. She can be mean at times, as her two older brothers will attest. She's energetic but deeply pessimistic. She has a crush on a boy named Cody, but a cheerleader named Heather already has won his affections.

Now Jodie is on an airplane to Egypt, as part of a school field trip. She saved money for the trip because she thinks she can somehow connect with her parents' spirit in this ancient land. She sits next to a middle-aged woman who reminds her of her mother. And they talk . . . and talk . . . and talk. In a way Jodie has never experienced, this woman is calming her down.

On this day, her sixteenth birthday and the eighth anniversary of her parents' death, Jodie just might have a chance to overcome her fear of losing someone close.

Then the pilot's voice crackles on the PA system. There's some trouble with the fuel tank or one of the engines . . . or something. Whatever the pilot says, people respond with panic. Now, just as Jodie has found a soul mate for the first time since her parents' death, the trip could end in tragedy.

What's Jodie going to do?

Answering the dossier's questions not only helped my students to create a vivid character. It also helped them to sketch out the arc of her story. The dossier helped us to see deep conflicts in the character, yearning to overcome tragedy. We also saw her youthful energy and *naiveté*, her independent spirit, and her need for connection. All the elements of a good story pop out when you complete a dossier.

The approach works for real-life characters too. This simple tool offers a can't-miss process for doing research on all the important characters of your story.

How much detail do you need? Depends. Longer, more complex stories require more detail for each question. You need not just simple answers, but the stories behind the answers.

Move from characterization to character and you have the makings of a real story.

The Idea Dossier offers a similar questionnaire on ideas, why they matter, where they come from, how they work, and more.

Problems and goals
- The problem are you trying to solve
- "Pain points," or why the present state of things is unacceptable (for someone)
- The ideal result
- What would happen if that result were to be achieved—or not
- What gets in the way of that ideal result—physical barriers, false or inadequate ideas, social or intellectual conventions, psychological cramping

---

Ideas and things

- The problem's *theoretical* elements, which involve *abstract* logic, definitions, analysis, and generalizations
- The problem's *empirical* elements, which are real, and physical, and tangible
- The categories you use to talk about these concerns
- The "boundaries" or "frames" of your problem or issue—in other words, what's *in* and what's *out* of your discussion
- The more (and less) fundamental of these matters

Qualities and relationships

- How to break down the key categories and ideas into smaller parts
- Possible ways to combine categories and ideas in new ways
- The important qualities of "real world" things—their size and scale, weight and density, color and texture, clarity and certainty, strength and flexibility?
- How these qualities be added and subtracted to these things
- What makes ideas and things stronger or weaker? More or less compelling as explanations?

The larger context
- How ideas relate to each other
- What ideas can be arranged in a hierarchy
- What ideas overlap, like circles in a Venn diagram—and what ideas *do not* interact or overlap
- How conflict and cooperation affect these things
- What conflict reveals about these ideas
- Which ideas or things are essential—that is, they can't be changed and they provide building blocks for everything else

Solving problems
- Understanding *causality*, or what causes what
- What kind of evidence is available to explore issues
- The reliability of that evidence

With these prompts, you can explore just about any problem imaginable. I am not the first person to think of such a tool. One of my favorites is a Soviet scientist and inventor named Genrich Altshuller, who invented a process known as TRIZ (the Russian acronym for Theory of Inventive Problem Solving). After studying more than 200,000 patents, Altshuller identified a number of simple questions to solve even the most complicated problems. Altshuller's technique is used in R&D departments the world over; its most famous user is the Korean electronics company Samsung.

#THE WHEEL OF CHARACTER TYPES

Every great story or analysis presents a whole cast of competing characters or ideas. How they interact with each other reveals the underlying tensions—and truths—of the piece.

The Wheel of Character Types contains four pairs of opposite types. You start with the hero and the villain, of course. Once you know what the hero wants—what his Holy Grail is—you can understand the villain. The villain, who often represents the rejected part of the hero, seeks to thwart the hero's quest. Other character oppositions, as you see here, include the Mentor and the Tempter, the Sidekick and the Skeptic, and the Heart and Mind.

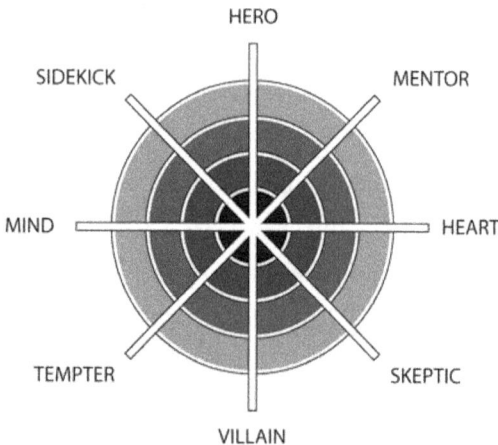

HERO

SIDEKICK

MENTOR

MIND

HEART

TEMPTER

SKEPTIC

VILLAIN

Good storytellers show the good and bad sides of both heroes and villains. We see the hero kick the dog. The hero of *It's a Wonderful Life*, George Bailey, sacrifices his every dream so that others can pursue theirs. But he can also be peevish. He makes sarcastic comments to friends, puts down the life work of his father, and snaps at his children. We also see the villain "save the cat." As Blake Snyder notes in his classic book on screenwriting, we need to see someone bad do something good, without any expectation of reward. We need to know that even the worst characters are complex, and we need to identify with them. So in the opening scene of *The Godfather*, the mobster Don Corleone pets a cat while making plans to murder and maim.

Think of it this way: Why would we want to explore a character who is completely evil or good? In fact, we would have little to explore—the answers would reveal themselves with every move.

Archetypical characters represent opposite tendencies of human character. Just as we have both heroic and villainous qualities, we have the other opposing tendencies too. We all have the wisdom of the mentor, but also the impulsiveness of the tempter. We have the loyalty of the sidekick and the negativity of the skeptic. We have the abstract intelligence of the mind and the emotional intelligence of the heart.

A good storyteller shows how characters wrestle with their many tendencies. All of us struggle because we do not understand ourselves fully. We all have blind spots. Our struggles bring out the complexity and drama of human life.

Books on human evolution call our species homo sapiens, Latin for "wise man." But we might better be known as homo narratus, for "storytelling beasts."

All communication begins and ends with stories. We are wired for storytelling. Lots of species use language. But as far as we know, only humans tell stories. Stories orient people in the world. Stories organize ideas and solve problems. Stories help us to increase our knowledge of the world.

Forty millennia ago, people recorded their stories for posterity on cave walls. Today, we share stories in books and on TV and in movies and on social media.

Whatever you want to say, you will say it better—and faster—if you use the basic structure of storytelling. The philosopher Aristotle described the basic structure of storytelling 2,500 years ago in *The Poetics*.

Stories, Aristotle notes, have three parts. In the beginning, we are shown the situation—the characters, the place, the issues. That's what I call the *world of the story*. Then, point by point, we see how the characters pursue their desires. At each stage, the characters encounter challenges—and, one way or another, address those challenges. That's what Aristotle calls the *rising action*. Finally, after addressing those barriers, the hero achieves something worthwhile (or fails trying). The story winds down. That's the *denouement.*

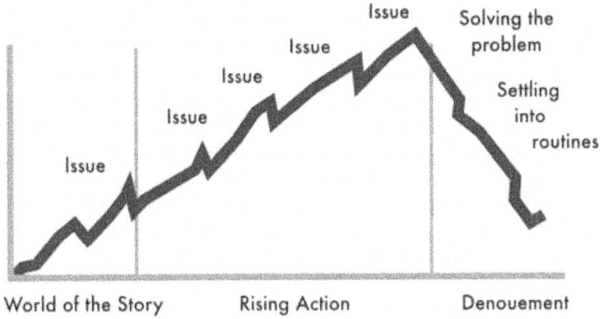

Aristotle called this basic structure the narrative arc. It looks like the trajectory of a ball thrown across a field. It rises slowly, reaches a peak, and then falls faster than it rose.

Want a good example of the Aristotelian narrative arc? Pull up a chair and listen to the adventure of Odysseus.

In the epic poem by Homer, we meet the hero as he seeks to return home to Ithaca and his wife Penelope after the Trojan War. As soon as Odysseus and his men leave Troy, they meet a phantasmagoric cast of foes and temptations from the seductions of Calypso and the Sirens to the terror of the Cyclops and the Laestrygonians to the twin dangers of Scylla and Charybdis. Odysseus takes on all of these dangers, one by one, each on its own terms. He uses his wisdom, cunning, and strength to understand the unique challenges that these foes pose. He finally returns home to face one last challenge. Suitors have taken over his home and Penelope feels growing pressure to accept Odysseus death and remarry. Odysseus uses his cunning, once again, to trounce the interlopers and restore his family.

Odysseus confronts his challenges, one by one. The difficulty of the challenges increases, as Odysseus journeys home, testing him in new ways. With every challenge, Odysseus gets that much closer to his goal— returning home and maturing as a man. Consider how we might plot *The Odyssey* on Aristotle's narrative arc:

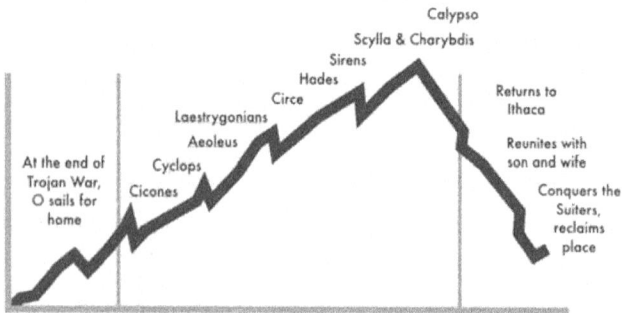

Embedded into every story is an argument or a point— sometimes known as the "moral of the story." The point of Odysseus's story is that struggle produces personal responsibility and growth.

Stories do not necessarily "prove" these arguments. But the timeless characters, their human flaws, their powerful drives, and their protean strength and creativity make these stories more persuasive than the tightest argument could ever be.

Let me make a couple final points about stories.

First, a well-wrought story touches readers emotionally. When you engage readers emotionally, you can engage them intellectually. Readers imagine themselves in the story—so they develop a stake in the issues you explore. Once you hook a reader with a story, you can discuss any issue.

Second, stories inhabit every level of writing. In every sentence, paragraph, section, and whole piece, we can give the reader a narrative experience—even if we're talking about abstract issues. I'll explain that later.

Any time you express yourself in a story, with characters struggling to overcome challenges, you have a chance to rivet your reader. That's the story.

....
#BEGINNINGS ...
....

> *Follow the advice of the King in*
> *Lewis Carroll's Alice in Wonderland:*
> *"Begin at the beginning, and go on till*
> *you come to the end: then stop."*

In the old days, before twenty-four-hour news cycles, reporters learned to present the five W's in every opening paragraph. The reader needed a quick overview of the story; the classic formula delivered.

When Japan attacked Pearl Harbor, *The New York Times* reported:

> Sudden and unexpected attacks [what] on
> Pearl Harbor, Honolulu [where], and other
> United States possessions in the Pacific [where]
> early yesterday [when] by the Japanese air
> force and navy [who] plunged the United
> States and Japan into active war [what].

Consider, for a moment, how well that opening paragraph informed readers about the facts and meaning of Pearl Harbor. Using vivid images, with concrete nouns and action verbs, the passage offers a complete overview of the news.

Nowadays, we learn about major news stories long before we read a newspaper. We hear about it on TV, radio, or the Internet. So we need a different kind of lead—one that takes us deep into the story, right away. Consider a handful of leads from recent winners of the Pulitzer Prize.

YOU ARE THERE: In her piece about the swift power of a tornado, Julia Keller of the *Chicago Tribune* gets the reader to see how much can happen in a short time by counting to ten:

> Ten seconds. Count it: One. Two. Three. Four.
> Five. Six. Seven. Eight. Nine. Ten. Ten seconds
> was roughly how long it lasted. Nobody had a
> stopwatch, nothing can be proven definitively,

but that's the consensus. The tornado that
swooped through Utica at 6:09 p.m. April 20
took some ten seconds to do what it did. Ten
seconds is barely a flicker. It's a long, deep
breath. It's no time at all. It's an eternity.

MAN-BITES-DOG: Rick Bragg shows sights that we
consider upside-down, in this case a man sewing, to
describe the culture of New Orleans during the recovery
from Hurricane Katrina:

> The little shotgun house is peeling and the
> Oldsmobile in front is missing a rear bumper,
> but Larry Bannock can glimpse glory through
> the eye of his needle. For almost a year he
> has hunkered over his sewing table, joining
> beads, velvet, rhinestones, sequins, feathers
> and ostrich plumes into a Mardi Gras costume
> that is part African, part Native American.

MYSTERY: Kenneth Weiss, a reporter for the *Los Angeles
Times*, treats the pervasive pollution of the oceans as a
thriller, with all the suspense of a John Le Carre novel:

> The fireweed began each spring as tufts of hairy
> growth spread across the seafloor fast enough
> to cover a football field in an hour. When
> fishermen touched it, their skin broke out in

searing welts. Their lips blistered and peeled. Their eyes burned and swelled shut. Water that splashed from their nets spread the inflammation to their legs and torsos. "It comes up like little boils," said Randolph Van Dyk, a fisherman whose powerful legs are pocked with scars. "At nighttime, you can feel them burning. I tried everything to get rid of them. Nothing worked."

FEELINGS: Writing in the Baltimore *Sun*, Diana Sugg uses her lead to develop empathy for the problem of stillbirth:

That chilly night in late October, the delivery room was so quiet. The doctor wrapped the 8-pound, 21-inch newborn girl in a pink-and-blue striped cotton blanket, pulled a matching cap over her brown hair and gently passed her to her mother. Margarete Heber cradled the baby. In the dim light, Heber could see the infant had her dark eyes, turned-up nose and distinctive chin. Perfect, except she was tinged blue. She had died just hours before she was born. Her birth would be her good-bye. "I am sorry," Heber whispered, kissing her stillborn daughter on the forehead. "I am so, so sorry."

SENSUAL POWER: Eric Newhouse of the *Great Falls Tribune* in Montana evokes the power of the senses — in this case, smell — to describe the pervasiveness of alcohol in American society:

> "When they put my baby on my breast, I knew something was wrong, so I lifted my head to look at him," Maza Weya said of her newborn. "I could smell the alcohol on his breath," she said. "My baby was born drunk." After years of drinking everything she could get her hands on, Maza Weya has managed to become sober. Her son isn't so lucky.

FISH OUT OF WATER: To illustrate the distractedness of everyday life, *The Washington Post*'s Gene Weingarten shows how few people notice when a virtuoso violinist works as a subway musician:

> He emerged from the Metro at the L'Enfant Plaza Station and positioned himself against a wall beside a trash basket. By most measures, he was nondescript: a youngish white man in jeans, a long-sleeved T-shirt and a Washington Nationals baseball cap. From a small case, he removed a violin. Placing the open case at his feet, he shrewdly threw in a few dollars and pocket change as seed money, swiveled it to face pedestrian traffic, and began to play.

Each of these leads puts the reader in a specific place. We get telling clues about the story's characters and struggles. We often see contradictions and surprises, which make us want to know more. Each of these leads makes us want to know more.

#. . . AND ENDINGS

If you have just one chance to make a first impression, as the old saying goes, you also have just one chance to make a lasting impression.

So don't blow the ending. Don't work hard to write clearly and concisely and then leave the reader in a boring haze at the end. Conclude your piece with an important point or image, helping the reader remember what you say.

As you approach the end of your piece—article, chapter, paper, book, speech, play, poem—ask what you want the reader to remember. Here are several possibilities:

CLINCH THE POINT: When you argue a point, you want to win. And you don't want to leave room for people to reach an opposite conclusion. So for most arguments, the conclusion offers an opportunity to clinch the point.

College students learn to clinch the point by reviewing their argument and its major points: "In this paper, I have demonstrated that . . ." That's fine. But you can also restate and clinch the point by painting a picture. If you leave the reader with something evocative, your argument will have greater staying power.

Here's how George Orwell concludes his 1946 essay "Politics and the English Language," which argues that lazy, sloppy writing can lead to tyranny:

> If you simplify your English, you are freed from the worst follies of orthodoxy. You cannot speak any of the necessary dialects, and when you make a stupid remark its stupidity will be obvious, even to yourself. Political language — and with variations this is true of all political parties, from Conservatives to Anarchists — is designed to make lies sound truthful and murder respectable, and to give an appearance of solidity to pure wind. One cannot change this all in a moment, but one can at least change one's own habits, and from time to time one can even, if one jeers loudly enough, send some worn-out and useless phrase — some *jackboot, Achilles' heel, hotbed, melting pot, acid test, veritable inferno*, or other lump of verbal refuse — into the dustbin, where it belongs.

Orwell leaves no doubt what he thinks about sloppy and clichéd language: It deserves to be eliminated like a stinking pail of garbage.

COME FULL CIRCLE: If the writer makes the reader a promise in the opening paragraphs, he can fulfill that promise in the closing paragraphs. Like Odysseus returning home, the piece finishes where it started.

In his classic 1959 essay "There is No News from Auschwitz" for *The New York Times*, A.M. Rosenthal opens: "The most terrible thing of all, somehow, was that at Brzezinka the sun was bright and warm, the rows of graceful poplars were lovely to look upon, and on the grass near the gates the children played." Rosenthal meditates on the Holocaust by considering the calm of one its horrific prison camps. And then he concludes: "There is nothing new to report about Auschwitz. It was a sunny day and the trees were green and at the gates the children played."

CREATE A FINAL IMAGE: Lots of stories end with a poignant scene of the characters in a new place. We experience closure when we see the problems of characters find resolution. We see how this resolution changes the world.

In *Sister Carrie*, the heroine takes a dizzying journey from innocence in a rural home in Wisconsin to worldliness and tragedy in big cities like Chicago, Montreal, and New York. At the end, Carrie Meeber has nothing left but the ruins of her life. Here's how Theodore Dreiser ends the story: "In your rocking chair, by your window dreaming, shall you long, alone. In your rocking chair, by your window, shall you dream such happiness as you may never feel."

Ernest Hemingway also ends *A Farewell to Arms* on a poignant note. Frederic Henry, the novel's narrator, has just said goodbye to Catherine in the hospital, where she hemorrhaged and died after losing a baby in childbirth. The novel ends: "After a while I went out and left the hospital and walked back to the hotel in the rain." That somber scene has become one of the most famous in American letters.

GLIMPSE THE FUTURE: You can also shoot the reader into the future, with speculation about what might happen to the characters. Toward the end of Mario Puzo's *The Godfather*, Michael Corleone holds his sister's baby during an elaborate Baptism ceremony; at the same time, his hit men carry out a series of murders, including the killing of the baby's father, who has betrayed the family. Afterward, when Michael's wife and sister confront him over the murder, he denies it. One by one, members of the family kiss his ring and acknowledge his status as the family's new boss. As one story ends, another begins.

At the end of Mark Twain's *Huckleberry Finn*, the narrator closes with his final plans for escape. "But I reckon I got to light out for the Territory ahead of the rest, because Aunt Sally she's going to adopt me and sivilize me and I can't stand it. I been there before."

Anton Chekhov's stories and plays almost always

end with a new beginning; they seem like setups for the *real* story. Consider these final lines (with story titles in parentheses):

> I set off for Petersburg that day, and I have not seen Dmitri Petrovitch nor his wife since. I am told that they are still living together. (*Terror*).

> And it seemed to them that they were within an inch of arriving at a decision, and that then a new, beautiful life would begin. And they both realized that the end was still far, far away, and that the hardest, the most complicated part was only just beginning. (*A Lady With Lapdog*).

> The day after this meeting I left Yalta and how Shamokhin's story ended I do not know. (*Ariadne*).

> What kind of life would it be? (*The Steppe*).

> 'Go-o-od-by-e,' shouted Samoylenko.
> 'There's no sight or sound of them,' said
> the deacon. 'Good luck on the journey!'
> It began to spot with rain. (*The Duel*).

> I pondered while the sun-scorched plain,
> the immense sky, the oak forest, dark on the
> horizon and the hazy distance, seemed saying

to me: 'Yes, there's no understanding anything
in this world! The sun began to rise.' (*Lights*)

Use irony and humor: "Life is easy," the British actor
Donald Wolfit said on his deathbed, "but comedy is
hard." Witty last words, eh?

Ironic endings say: *Hey, this might not make sense,
but it's how things go sometimes.* Closing with irony, you
show that not all stories can be tied up neatly. Sometimes
questions cannot be answered. Sometimes doubt needs
to remain.

In a piece on the chess master Bobby Fischer, Bill
Nack searches for the reclusive and mad genius. Nack
interviews old friends, who cannot help. When he learns
that Fischer uses the Los Angeles Public Library, Nack
prowls near the card catalogues and current periodicals
room. One day, after months of searching, he sees his
man. He follows him out the library and down the street.
But he cannot bring himself to approach Fischer.

> I finally had him in my sights, and I simply could
> not bring myself to reach out a hand to shake
> his. Fischer had chosen this life of privacy and
> seclusion, for whatever reason, and to breach it
> now seemed a pointless intrusion. ... I chased
> him for block after block through the streets of
> Los Angeles ... The last time I saw him, he was
> standing there under a large clock hung upon

the corner of a building. Fittingly enough, the clock was broken, its hands motionless on the dial. Then he disappeared into a group of people climbing on Bus 483, bound for Pasadena.

Nack now knew what he needed to know. He needed to halt his own obsession with a man whose brilliant mind had degenerated into hatred and paranoia. So, having captured his quarry, Nack let him go.

Sometimes you want to leave the reader with a smile, to emphasize the absurdity of the vanity fair that is modern life. Or you want to make fun of your role of writer.

In one essay, the humorist Roy Blount explores the smiles of politicians – smiles that were fake, contrived, scared, jubilant, confident, shifty. To close his ruminations, he reflects on the disappearance of Jimmy Carter's famous grin:

I don't know whether you have noticed, but by the time of the Iran crisis, that old peculiar grin of his was gone. The pressures of his office and his jogging and his sufferance of all those wild redneck Iranians had given him a more truly hurt-looking austerity. He looked like he could reach a little deeper and come up with some real country music.

For Blount, authenticity comes down to whether you can sing country. When Carter lost his trademark grin, he gained something deeper.

At the end of *If On a Winter's Night a Traveler*, Italo Calvino plays with the writer-reader relationship. He shows a couple in bed, reading. The wife finishes her bed and bids her husband to turn off the light. "Just a moment," he says, "I've almost finished *If On a Winter's Night a Traveler* by Italo Calvino."

OFFER AN AFTERWARD: At the end of our piece, we might like to offer some additional thoughts as a post-script. Histories, biographies, memoirs, even novels often use an afterward to place the story in a larger context. Movies like based on true events, *Erin Brockovich* and *We are Marshall*, almost always tell "the rest of the story" right before credits.

....
#BOOKENDS
....

> *For every piece you write*
> *—anything longer than, say,*
> *300 words—start by writing the*
> *first and last paragraphs.*

Years ago, I fell behind on a project. I was writing a book about the 1963 March on Washington, which came out in 2010 under the title *Nobody Turn Me Around*. The deadline was approaching, but I had only written a few chapters. I had to start making progress—fast.

When I sat down to compose, I tried to write a whole scene at once, from the beginning to the end. By the third or fourth paragraph, I was stuck. I started to ramble. I had no direction.

Then I had a thought: I always tell students to "start strong, finish strong." Maybe, just maybe, I should follow my own advice.

So I went through my notes and wrote the first and last paragraph for about ten or eleven chapters. I made no effort to write the middle paragraphs—just the start and the finish.

I started by considering how to hook the reader. I imagined the first moments in a scene in a film or a TV show—the way the camera establishes the setting, with the characters and location.

Then I imagine how I wanted to leave the reader – and what kind of final image or idea I wanted to offer. Whatever issue arose in the first paragraph, how would we know when the characters had settled (or failed to settle) that issue? What was the "fadeout" moment I wanted to offer readers?

To explain how it worked, let me tell you about the book's prologue, which describes three black teenagers who hitchhike from Gadsden, Alabama, to attend the March on Washington. The three had devoted the summer to the movement, protesting at home, in other cities in the South, and in New York. At the end of the summer, they wanted to go to the March but didn't have the money to pay for the bus trip. So they convinced their parents to let them hitchhike to Washington. Here's the first paragraph:

> On a pitch-black night, a crescent moon
> barely visible in the sky, three teenaged
> boys walked along the gentle slopes of
> Highland Avenue on the edge of Lookout
> Mountain, then to U.S. Highway 11, north
> of their hometown of Gadsden, Alabama.

This was the beginning of the long journey. I could have opened the story at some other moment—earlier in the day when the boys got the idea to hitchhike, or maybe later on the journey or arriving in D.C. But I decided the best starting point would be that moment of truth, when they actually took the risk and set out their hike.

Now take a look at the closing paragraph:

> On August 28, 1963, hundreds of thousands of
> demonstrators would carry those signs down
> constitution and Independence avenues and what
> Martin Luther King called the greatest demon-
> stration for freedom in the nation's history.

I end where the larger story begins—with the three Gadsden teens in Washington as the March of Washington is about to begin.

Between these two paragraphs, I not only told the story of the Gadsden boys, their involvement in the movement, how they got to D.C., and their volunteer work in the days before the March. I also provided background information on the civil rights movement and the events of 1963, so the reader could understand why the March was so important—and also why the stories of ordinary activists was so important to the movement.

Once I wrote these bookend paragraphs, it was easy to fill in the paragraphs in between. I started to think of those middle paragraphs as the stones on the path.

A simple but powerful truth: Once you know your starting point and destination, it's easy to figure out what steps are necessary to make the trip.

#BEATS

Create scenes and summaries that move back and forth, dialectically, from one idea to another. Generate tension—and raise the stakes—with a series of conflicts that clarify the stakes of the game.

Think back on the scenes in your life—and in books and movies, and even in songs and sports—that riveted your attention.

Now try to remember how people interacted in those scenes. One person acted, the other reacted, the first person responded, a third entered the fray, the first two responded. Back and forth, the characters hit ideas back and forth like tennis balls. Each volley created new possibilities, with suspense. The longer the volleys, the greater the stakes and the tension.

Hollywood has a term for this rat-a-tat-tat exchange —*beats*. A beat is any action, however small, that changes the story or argument and propels it forward. A scene from a Hollywood movie typically contains twelve to twenty beats; the whole movie has 500 to 1,000 beats.

In a well-constructed scene, beats keep the audience riveted. Every action raises a question; every response, in turn, raises a new question. Dialogue, actions, gestures, descriptions, and details—all act like beats, creating a sense of anticipation.

Think, for a moment, of the exquisitely awful debate between Macbeth and Lady Macbeth in the hour before Macbeth kills King Duncan. Lady Macbeth wants her husband to kill the king so he can claim the throne himself. Macbeth wants to be king, but he hesitates to kill Duncan. So Lady Macbeth seduces, bullies, and shames him into doing it. See how it happens:

1. **Doubt**: Alone, Macbeth debates the assassination plan. He's conflicted.

2. **Decision**: When Lady Macbeth arrives, Macbeth says he wants to back out of the plan. "We will proceed no further in this business," he says.

3. **Attack**: Lady Macbeth shames him, questioning his ambition and manhood, calling him "green and pale." She wonders: "Art thou afeard to be the same in thine own act and valor as thou art in desire?" She asks if he wants to "live a coward in thine own esteem."

4. **Plea**: Macbeth begs her to stop: "Prithee, peace!" The true test of manhood, he argues, is doing the right thing: "I dare do all that may become a man; who dares do more is none."

5. **Harsher attack**: Now Lady Macbeth really lays into him. You agreed to this! Now you're backing out? Angrily, she says she would "dash the brains" of a nursing baby before she would dare back out of the plan.

6. **Question**: "If we should fail?" Macbeth asks lamely.

7. **Response**: "We fail!" she says. "But screw your courage to the sticking-place, and we'll not fail."

8. **Strategy**: Then she instructs him how to kill Duncan. Wait till he's sleeping, get his guards drunk, then frame them for the murder.

9. **Retreat**: Macbeth relents. Duncan's guards, "mark'd with blood," will get blamed, Macbeth agrees.

10. **Reassurance**: No one, Lady Macbeth assures him, will suspect the real culprits. "We shall make our griefs and clamor roar upon his death."

11. **Resolve**: In that case, Macbeth says, "I am settled." He has resolved to commit murder.

For whatever Macbeth says, his wife has a response. Moving back and forth, from one character to the other, Shakespeare escalates the tension. He shows Lady Macbeth's power over her husband. For every plea, she responds with some kind of manipulation. And she shows her utter heartlessness with the plan to frame Duncan's guards.

All great scenes move back and forth like this. Each beat moves the action forward. Each beat raises the stakes. Each beat matters.

The concept of the beat, which comes from theater, also offers a useful technique for non-narrative writing. Beats offer a way to set up a point, consider alternatives, and move the discussion forward. Beats, then, take this form: *You may think X, but actually Y.* After luring the reader with one expectation, you respond with something surprising.

*You may think civil service removed politics
from bureaucracy, but actually...*

*You may think that the brain is permanently
hardwired in infancy, but actually ...*

*You may think cutting taxes
reduces revenues, but actually ...*

*You may think banning alcohol to
minors reduces drinking, but actually ...*

*You may think that the lethal danger of
AIDS reduces risky behavior, but actually ...*

These arguments set up a clash of different explanations. We move back and forth between the supporting ideas of both sides.

Whatever the genre—storytelling or argument—beats offer a way to create tempo and highlight different angles of a problem. You nudge the reader toward X, and then surprise him with an assertion of Y. You look at Y in a new light, then surprise him with Z.

One last point: Beats offer a useful way to test writing. If a beat changes a story, in useful ways, it belongs. If it doesn't, if it's a meaningless detail, then it does not belong. When you get in the habit of testing beats, you can carry that habit to other parts of your writing. Does the quotation add to the story—*change* the story—in a useful way? Does a statistic? A piece of historical background? A detail about a character's appearance or mannerisms?

Like the beats in a movie or song, every phrase or sentence you write should respond to what happened before and set up what follows. Every passage should offer something new, even surprising.

···

#QUESTIONS
···

Inquire about everything you see,
hear, think, and feel—deliberately,
with an unclogged mind.

We ask questions all the time. We can't help it. Socrates said: "I have a notion that, when the mind is thinking, it is simply talking to itself, asking questions and answering them." We have a hard time stopping.

The point is to ask the right kinds of questions.

If you have a good question, you can build a strong story, explanation, or argument. You know what kinds of issues to explore, what kinds of people to interview, what kinds of background research you need to do.

Just as important, you know what issues *not* to explore. Too often, we often get so interested in the side stories that we veer off course. To stay on course, you need to remind yourself of the question. Otherwise, you will get overwhelmed with extraneous material and write a confused piece.

Paradoxically, the sharper your question, the more information you will find. With a focused topic, you know what information to look for—and that information is easy to spot when you go looking. Searching for information about a broad topic is harder, because it gets lost in piles of unhelpful information. It's the difference between looking for a needle in a haystack and looking for a needle in a sewing kit.

Language mavens tell us there are two kinds of questions—either/or questions and *w*- questions. Either/or questions offer specific options and ask to choose one: "Who is the better writer—Hemingway or Fitzgerald?" *W* questions begin with the words who, what, when, where, or why.

Questions explore how our world works. What motivates a character? What's the major issue in designing a good health care system? What are the limits of free speech in a democracy? How will the Internet affect the process of gathering news? What makes a successful baseball team? How can children be motivated to learn? How can addicts overcome their biological and psychological need for alcohol or drugs?

You *really* start to understand these issues when you ask follow up questions. I might ask: What qualities make a person an expert? You might answer intelligence and hard work. Fair enough, but what do we mean by "intelligence"? Logic? Knowledge? Skills? And how do we measure these capacities? What other qualities strengthen intelligence? Disposition? Interest? And what does "hard work" mean? Does it mean putting in long hours? Keeping a regular schedule? Working without distraction? The more followup questions we ask, the sharper our thinking gets.

So how do you come up with a good question? The best way, in my experience, is to write down everything you know about your topic. Put it all on one piece of paper. That's critical. If you need a big piece of paper, that's fine. Just be sure to put everything on one sheet, so you can see every idea that comes to mind.

How do you arrange these ideas on the sheet? Any way you like. Some writers group similar ideas together; others show connections between opposites. Some writers list data in one part of the sheet and general ideas or principles in another; others cluster major concepts with specific data. Always—*always*—draw diagrams and lines to make connections among ideas and data.

Students of intelligence, increasingly, have used "divergence tests" to assess a person's ability to think. If I asked you to name all the possible uses of a book, you might mention reading material, cutouts for posters, doorstop, and a good to be bartered and sold. But you would show *real* creativity if you could add to that obvious list. You could add to the list: kindling, weapon, writing surface, straight edge, fan, noisemaker, blotter, coaster, Rorschach, symbol. You could spend an hour playing this game. The more you played, the more creative your ideas would be.

That's the goal of brainstorming your topic. The

more ideas you spill on your page, the more questions pop off the page. When you see questions, you have the potential to see patterns.

All writing, in one way or another, seeks to solve riddles. Stories do so dramatically, focusing on one-and-only people, events, places, and times. Analyses do so logically and empirically, gathering information on large sets of similar things.

Whodunit? What causes what? "Whodunit?" is the classic question of mystery stories. Someone committed a crime and the detective works to uncover the culprit. Seeking out leads, interviewing people who knew the victim, sorting the motives and evidence, the detective eventually isolates the doer of the deed.

"What causes what?" is the classic question of science and analysis. Some event occurs and the researcher works to identify what caused the outcome. Just as the detective identifies and assesses possible suspects, the researcher identifies variables.

The difference between stories and analysis is simple. Stories focus on one-and-only people, events, times, and places—like the murderer and the victim and the people in his life, and, of course, the detective. Analysis focuses on many-times-over phenomena—like a whole set of crimes and what kinds of things *usually, in general,* happen to cause the crimes.

Analytic writers make generalizations. Whatever topic you're trying to understand—poverty, presidential power, autism, family dynamics, planning, or health – involves: lots of variables. Consider the problem of obesity in America. What variables might explain why people get morbidly overweight?

1. Genetics
2. Inadequate exercise
3. Poor nutrition
4. Inadequate sleep
5. Empty calories, from candy bars to pasta to beer
6. Sedentary lifestyles—too much screen time, not enough engagement with the real world
7. Depression
8. Chemical imbalances
9. Changing metabolism
10. Stress

Research shows that all of these variables play a part. The question then becomes: How much?

To find out, you need to *operationalize* these variables. That's the word scientists use to describe what they measure. To operationalize genetics, you might track a person's family history or get genetic testing to identify changes in chromosomes, genes, or proteins. To operationalize exercise, you might keep records about physical activity (walking, standing, running, swimming, playing sports, and so on) and inactivity (sitting at a desk or on a sofa). To operationalize nutrition, you might track all the food and dietary supplements, with detailed information about different kinds of macronutrients and micronutrients.

You get the idea.

Once you have gathered data for all your variables, you can start to undertake statistical analysis. Analysis checks each variable to determine whether it produces some change. You do that by "isolating the variables"— seeing what happens when one variable changes but the others remain the same.

Statistics, it sometimes seems, have taken over our world—from the "Moneyball" strategies in sports to the complex algorithms that fuel the Internet. As an analyst, your job is to pluck out and explain the numbers that offer the greatest insight.

Part 2

Building blocks

How many different kinds of structures could you create with six Lego bricks?

That's a puzzle that mathematicians have been debating for years. In 1972, the Lego company advertised that six of the standard Lego bricks—with eight studs—would create 102,981,500 different formations.

But Soren Eilers, a professor at the University of Copenhagen, was skeptical. He noticed that Lego's math was based on stacking the bricks into towers. What if the Legos could be attached into flatter structures? The number of structures multiplied. He wrote a computer program to calculate the number of structures that extend wide as well as tall. The program calculated that six Lego bricks could be combined in 915,103,765 ways.

So what are the building blocks of the English language? You might nominate the 26 letters of the alphabet, which can be combined in endless ways to produce words. Or you might nominate words, which also can then be combined in endless ways to produce sentences and paragraphs. Amazing. *Mind-bending.*

But I think of sentences and paragraphs as the ultimate Lego blocks of writing. Why? As writers, we build *ideas* with our bricks. The most basic expression of an idea is the sentence. The most basic development of an idea is the paragraph.

Or think of it this way: If you can build a great sentence, you can build anything. Right away, you can build two, three, four, and more sentences. Then you can create great paragraphs. And then, your expression knows no bounds. You can create essays, stories, explanations, arguments, poems, plays, songs—absolutely anything.

But first you have to master the art of the sentence and the paragraph. I'm going to show you how.

....
#SENTENCING
....

> *Get right to the point—usually.*
> *Sometimes, to orient your reader*
> *or provide variety, you can provide*
> *background or "setup" information*
> *first. But get to the point before*
> *you lose your reader.*

The classic advice for all writers goes like this: *Say who does what to whom.* In other words, tell the reader the subject (who or what), the verb (the action), and the object (the person or thing acted upon). Or: *Subject-Verb-Object.* Or: *S-V-O.* Not every action has an object, so we might simplify the idea thus: *Who does what?* That's S-V, in shorthand.

The subject and verb create the core of your

sentences. Athletes know they need strong cores—the abdomen—because they need to transfer power from the legs and butt up to the upper body. If the core is weak, the athlete cannot use his limbs powerfully. The same concept applies to writing sentences. Without a strong core, the rest of the sentence falters.

Take a look at three masters of prose and how often they start sentences with the subject and verb:

> You expected to be sad in the fall. Part of you died each year when the leaves fell from the trees and their branches were bare against the wind and the cold, wintery light. But you knew there would always be the spring, as you knew the river would flow again after it was frozen. When the cold rains kept on and killed the spring, it was as though a young person died for no reason.
>
> —**Ernest Hemingway**, *A Moveable Feast*

> I am an expression of the divine, just like a peach is, just like a fish is. I have a right to be this way...I can't apologize for that, nor can I change it, nor do I want to... We will never have to be other than who we are in order to be successful... We realize that we are as ourselves unlimited and our experiences valid. It is for the rest of the world to recognize this, if they choose.
>
> —**Alice Walker**, *The Color Purple*

She has the sort of body you go to see in marble. She has golden hair. Quickly, deftly, she reaches with both hands behind her back and unclasps her top. Setting it on her lap, she swivels ninety degrees to face the towboat square. Shoulders back, cheeks high, she holds her pose without retreat. In her ample presentation there is defiance of gravity. There is no angle of repose. She is a siren and these are her songs.

—**John McPhee**, *Uncommon Carriers*

You could do worse than to imitate these masters. Find passages that use a strong "core" and copy them into your notebook. Then write your own sentences, imitating their syntax, detail for detail. Practicing good form helps wire your brain to use that good form on your own.

Of course, giving every sentence an S-V-O format—or even beginning every sentence with S-V—could get monotonous. Like water torture—*drip, drip, drip*—such regularity can become irritating. Take a look at the opening of Dan Pope's novel *In the Cherry Tree*:

Summer days began without a plan. You got up. You had a bowl of cereal. You went outside. A lawnmower hummed. Ducks passed overhead in perfect V formation like World War II bombers. The dog barked, and another dog barked back. Someone was hammering nails into a roof.

Someone was bouncing a basketball two streets away. You heard the sound, then the echo. A cat crept across the grass and disappeared beneath the hedge. It was hot. The sun was strong. The crickets made a seething noise. The sprinkler came on and made a quiet rain sound when the water hit the grass and then a louder rain sound when the water hit the street.

On and on he goes: Subject-Verb-Object. Thankfully, a few longer sentences offer relief from the drip, drip, drip. But we need more variety.

The lesson: So don't begin *every* sentence with the subject and verb. Sometimes start with context or background. By delaying the action just a bit—saying a thing or two before Subject-Verb-Object—you allow the reader to get oriented. You can offer four major kinds of context before getting to S-V-O:

- *Antecedents*: To set up the present action, say what happened before. Adjusting Pope slightly, then, we might write: "After you got up and ate a bowl of cereal, you went outside."
- *Setting*: To provide a sense of context, step back and provide the broader setting for the action. Another Pope adjustment: "In that hot, sticky summer air, with the sun beating down, you could hear the crickets make a seething noise."

- *Ideas*: To make sense of the action, provide a concept. Pope adjusted again: "In these days of endless hours doing nothing, when our worries were confined to silly feuds and the desire to put off fall forever…"

- *Attribution*: To gain credibility, say where you got your information. The final Pope adjustment: "According to The Dad's remembrances, which he shared any time we climbed the tree to the orchard, the apple trees were planted in neat rows that went up the hill as far as you could see."

Starting with the subject and verb is a good habit. You can bet your Scrabble Q tile that Dan Pope never loses readers with long, meandering digressions. But he *might* annoy readers with his rat-a-tat-tat style. With a touch of variety, Pope would give readers the pacing they need. Readers need clarity and predictability—but they also need variety and surprise.

....
#LINES
....

> *Whatever shape you choose,*
> *write your piece line by line.*

Years ago, I was teaching writing at Yale University. I taught my students the importance of starting and finishing their sentences strongly. Our class mantra was: "Start strong, finish strong." They understood the need to grab the reader, right away. They also knew the importance of finishing every sentence with a bang.

Why is it so important to start and finish strongly? Because that's what people pay the most attention—and what they remember most. So you need to take advantage of that attention.

So what do I mean by start strong? Think of the old expression: You only have one chance to make a good first impression. When you start strong—in a sentence, paragraph, or whole piece—you make a strong impression. You grab the reader. You make a connection. And that's what writing is all about. So what do I mean by start strong? Two things:

- Say what happens—usually who does what.
- Set up the action—usually by describing the moment, sometimes by describing an idea essential to understanding the rest of the sentence.

Now what about finishing strong? What does that mean? As psychologists note, people need a sense of closure before they are comfortable moving on. They want to make sense of their experiences. So by the end of your pieces, do one of two things:

- "Make it a wrap"—that is, complete your thought.
- Leave the reader with a compelling question or image that moves the reader into the next stage of your writing.

What, you may ask, about the middle? All the words between the middle and end perform two basic tasks:

- Describe the steps you need to get from the beginning to the end—a sequence of actions or thoughts.
- Provide attribution for what happens in the sentence—the reason you know what you say you know.

Now let's return to my brainy Yale students.

In our class discussions, they clearly understood the imperative to "start strong, finish strong." But they continued to write sentences that meandered at the start and ended with a whimper. Clearly, *understanding* a concept is not the same thing as *using* that concept. What could I do? How could I get my students to actually practice what I preached? One day I had a brainstorm. I gave them a new rule. When they composed their papers, I told them to use the landscape (horizontal) view for their document, not the standard portrait (vertical) view.

Almost always, you know right away whether a sentence starts and ends strongly—if you ask yourself. The landscape view, with the line-by-line formatting, makes that easy. To see if you start strongly, just run your finger down them left side of the page, line by line. To see if you end strongly, run your finger down the right side of the page, line by line. It's easy to spot clunkers when you can find the beginnings and endings so quickly.

When my students turned in their papers, I asked them what they thought of our experiment. They loved it. They said it made writing easier. It made editing *a lot* easier. And the papers were much better—much easier to read and understand. In previous batches of papers, I always encountered at least a few dozen sentences that I did not understand, at least right away. With this new batch, I understood every single sentence, right away.

One of my students added a final thought that I will always remember.

"It looks like poetry," she said, holding up her paper with its array of jagged lines.

And it does. That, it turns out, is the most important point of all. The landscape view makes it easy to pay close attention to each line, one after another. And when you do that, you are on your way to writing well.

Line by line, you focus on writing one strong sentence after another. If you can write one strong sentence, you can write two or three or more. And then, you can write anything.

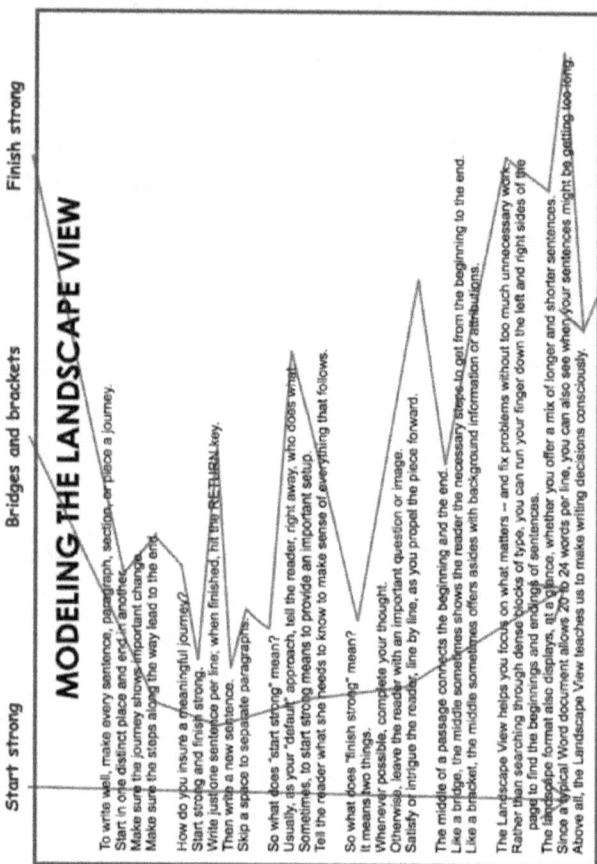

MODELING THE LANDSCAPE VIEW

Start strong · Bridges and brackets · Finish strong

To write well, make every sentence, paragraph, section, or piece a journey.
Start in one distinct place and end in another.
Make sure the journey shows important change.
Make sure the steps along the way lead to the end.

How do you insure a meaningful journey?
Start strong and finish strong.
Write just one sentence per line; when finished, hit the RETURN key.
Then write a new sentence.
Skip a space to separate paragraphs.

So what does "start strong" mean?
Usually, as your "default" approach, tell the reader, right away, who does what.
Sometimes, to start strong means to provide an important setup.
Tell the reader what she needs to know to make sense of everything that follows.

So what does "finish strong" mean?
It means two things.
Whenever possible, complete your thought.
Otherwise, leave the reader with an important question or image.
Satisfy or intrigue the reader, line by line, as you propel the piece forward.

The middle of a passage connects the beginning and the end.
Like a bridge, the middle sometimes shows the reader the necessary steps to get from the beginning to the end.
Like a bracket, the middle sometimes offers asides with background information or attributions.

The Landscape View helps you focus on what matters -- and fix problems without too much unnecessary work.
Rather than searching through dense blocks of type, you can run your finger down the left and right sides of the page to find the beginnings and endings of sentences.
The landscape format also displays, at a glance, whether you offer a mix of longer and shorter sentences.
Since a typical Word document allows 20 to 24 words per line, you can also see when your sentences might be getting too long.
Above all, the Landscape View teaches us to make writing decisions consciously.

*Use hinges—words that create a pause,
with an opportunity for elaboration
—somewhere near the middle.*

Kids growing up in the 1970s and 1980s remember the song "Conjunction Junction." The song played in cartoon series called *Schoolhouse Rock*, which aired during Saturday morning cartoons on TV. The song started like this:

> Conjunction Junction, what's your function?
> Conjunction Junction, how's that function?
> I got three favorite cars
> That get most of my job done
> Conjunction Junction, what's their function?
> I got "and", "but", and "or"
> They'll get you pretty far.

It was a great way to learn the basic part of speech—the conjunction, which connects clauses and coordinates words within a clause. Conjunctions include not just the Big Three—*and, but*, and *or*—but also *for, nor, yet*, and *so*. Conjunctions provide the "connective tissue" that helps words express complete thoughts.

Some conjunctions (known as "correlative") operate as pairs to join words or groups of words in a sentence.

Those correlatives include *either/or, not only/but also, neither/nor, both/and, whether/or, just as/so, as much/as, no sooner/than*, and *rather/than*. So we might say:

> Leila would choose either Virginia or Bucknell as her college.
>
> Bill Buckley excelled at not only political commentary, but also sailing and playing the harpsichord.
>
> The popularity of the *Star Wars* movies reflected both Americans' belief in heroism and their desire for an adventure with ambiguity.
>
> Sam no sooner arrived at the airport than the airlines cancelled its flights.

Other conjunctions ("subordinating") join together independent and dependent clauses. Independent clauses, of course, express complete thoughts and can stand alone as complete sentences. Dependent clauses cannot stand alone; they lack either a noun or verb. Consider this example of a sentence with independent and dependent clauses:

> By winning the World Series in 2015, the Kansas City Royals proved that even teams from small cities could dominate the game.

The clause beginning with "By winning," cannot stand alone; the clause beginning "the Kansas City Royals" can stand alone as a complete thought.

The most common subordinating conjunctions include *after*, *although*, *as*, *as far as*, *as if*, *as long as*, *as soon as*, *as though*, *because*, *before*, *even if*, *even though*, *every time*, *if*, *in order that*, *since*, *so*, *so that*, *than*, *though*, *unless*, *until*, *when*, *whenever*, *where*, *whereas*, *wherever*, and *while*.

Are you still with me? Good, because here comes the payoff.

The best way to master writing is use conjunctions. Short sentences offer the basic unit of all writing, but that's not always enough. The ultimate goal of good writing is to *show relationships*. We want to see how characters, events, ideas, and evidence *relate* to each other. So you need a hinge connecting one idea with another.

Young writers often struggle to write well—and concisely—because they write too short or too long. Uninspired, they blurt out cold, uninteresting sentences: *The president is the leader. … Tom Brady didn't cheat … Jay Z is cool. … I'm tired.* Or they ramble on forever, without a point: *I know for a fact that Tom Brady didn't cheat because he's awesome and has won lots of Super Bowls and is very popular in New England.*

Writing with conjunctions forces you to relate ideas that are worth relating. Just ask the teachers and students of New Dorp High School in Staten Island, New York.

For years, students struggled to write even rudimentary sentences well. The school regularly finished among the poorest achieving schools in the state. Four out of ten students dropped out before graduation.

To transform the system, teachers decided to make writing a central part of all subjects. No one knew what specific techniques would help students to write well. So teachers started examining student papers for clues. What made a paper good? Was it intelligence? Or effort? Or good reading skills? No, no, and no. Finally, one teacher found the answer. Poor writers used short, disjointed sentences; good writers used complex sentences.

Thus was born the strategy of hinges. And, I am happy to report, the performance of students at New Dorp improved dramatically—in all subjects. When students were prompted to connect two thoughts with a hinge, they thought better and write better. Hinges force us to express complex ideas, without meandering off on a tangent.

So consider this a prompt: *Use hinges in your writing.*

#PARAGRAPHING

For every paragraph, express and develop just one idea. Give that expression the form of a narrative arc. Start by introducing the idea. Then

develop the idea, point by point.
Then end with a satisfying conclusion.

If the sentence is the most important unit of writing, the paragraph is a close runner up. The paragraph gives your sentences form. Just as an athlete needs to bring together a number of separate motions into a single action—like throwing a ball—a writer needs to bring together discrete sentences into paragraphs. Paragraphs connect ideas into bigger pieces. Paragraphs allow us to see how different ideas relate to each other.

Funny, then, that so few people—even writers—can even say what a paragraph is. Even rock-star linguists, like Harvard's Steven Pinker, cannot offer a working definition of a paragraph. In his book on writing, Pinker even denies that a paragraph serves any purpose besides offering occasional breaks in the writing. In *The Sense of Style*, Pinker writes: "Many writing guides provide detailed instructions on how to build a paragraph. But the instructions are misguided, because there is no such thing as a paragraph." The paragraph, Pinker says, offers nothing more than "a visual bookmark that allows the reader to pause." In sum, a paragraph is what you want it to be.

But that's a copout. We can do better. Try this working definition: *A paragraph is the statement and development of a single idea.*

All too often, when we first begin writing a passage, our thoughts spill out, one after another. We begin with one thought and then, without developing it, jump to another thought. And so paragraphs become jumbles of thoughts, some developed and some not. After a while, we hit the return key. We think we have written a paragraph just because we have created, as Pinker says, a brief pause.

To avoid catch-all paragraphs, consider the concept of the "idea bucket." Every paragraph is a bucket; every bucket contains just one idea, along with whatever information are needed to develop that idea. Each paragraph can stand alone.

So how do you make sure you don't write paragraphs that meander off in different directions?

The answer is simple. As you write—or after you have written a passage—create a short label for each idea. If you find more than one idea in a paragraph, break it up into as many paragraphs as ideas. Delete the ideas that do not address the topic.

Take a look at this paragraph:

Alexandra Ferguson started making pillows in her living room in New York and found buyers on the craft site Etsy. She found a market for pillows decorated with bold letters—LOL, XOXO, MERDE, THE GOOD LIFE, GO TO THE GYM, READY FOR WHATEVER, ASK YOUR DAD, EAT YOUR VEGGIES, and more. Ferguson's Etsy site now includes 75 different pillows, which you can order online. If you want pillows with custom words, you can order them too. Over time her business grew so fast that she opened a factory in a Brooklyn complex called Industry City. Ferguson is surrounded with other craft people, from clothing to woodworking to artisanal food producers. Over the years, Brooklyn has become the "it" place because of its growing cluster of small startups. Ferguson's pillows are used in dens, dorm rooms, bedrooms, and anywhere people want a "light touch." Ferguson says she expects to add three employees to her current staff of nine. Her greatest challenge, she says, is finding workers with accurate and fast sewing skills.

Now identify the ideas in that paragraph. I count three:

- Alexandra's pillows
- Alexandra's business
- A community of creative people

When you throw all these ideas into one paragraph, you get lost and confused. You lose sight of what you want to say. What's the point here? Is it the product that Alexandra Ferguson makes? Or her factory and business? Or the community where she lives? Each idea deserves its own treatment. So label the ideas and break up the paragraph, like this—

Alexandra Ferguson makes colorful, whimsical pillows for sale on Etsy. She found a market for pills decorated with bold letters—lol, xoxo, merde, the good life, go to the gym, ready for whatever, ask your dad, eat your beggies, and more. If you want pillows with custom words, you can order them too. The pillows are used in dens, dorm rooms, bedrooms, and anywhere people want a "light touch."

Ferguson's started making pillows in her living room in New York and found buyers on the craft site Etsy. She now sells 75 different pillows on the site. Over time her business grew so fast that she opened a factory in a Brooklyn complex called Industry City. Ferguson says she expects to add three employees to her current staff of nine. Her greatest challenge, she says, is finding workers with accurate and fast sewing skills.

Ferguson is surrounded with other craft people, from clothing to woodworking to artisanal food producers. Over the years, Brooklyn has become the "it" place because of its growing cluster of small startups.

Look at strong writers over the past century—Ernest Hemingway, Scott Fitzgerald, Eudora Welty, Gay Talese,

Elizabeth Gilbert, Laura Hillenbrand—and you see that they follow the one-idea rule. Each paragraph is a mini-essay, a complete expression of a single idea, which follows the previous idea and sets up the next.

A piece of writing, then, is a string of buckets. When you label all the ideas/paragraphs, you see instantly how well the ideas move from the beginning to the end of the piece. As a general rule, one idea should lead to the next. You can take digressions; sometimes digressions offer important insight. But somehow you need to get back on the main road. Idea labeling helps to do just that.

··

#ANTISESQUIPEDILIANISM
··

Use the simplest possible words to make your point. Save the Ph.D. vocabulary for Ph.D. ideas. Even then, translate those big concepts into basic English.

"Everything," Albert Einstein once said, "should be made as simple as possible—but not simpler."

The writer's job is to simplify reality for the reader. Out of the "blooming, buzzing confusion" of the world, the writer creates a space where the reader can pay attention to one thing at a time. Distraction and confusion pose the biggest threats to that attention. When the reader gets disoriented, you have lost her—and you might not get her back.

That's why you need to use simple words. Rather than dazzle your readers, explain in terms everyone can understand. Avoid the brain cramps—moments of confusion or disorientation—that come with long, obscure words.

All too often, writers want to be writerly—that is, they want to show off their command of language. They want to show that they can express ideas better than non-writers. And so they haul out a thesaurus and use complex, obscure words when a simple word works better. They think that an exotic vocabulary makes them look brighter. In fact, this kind of showing off makes them look dimmer. That's what Princeton psychologist Daniel Oppenheimer found in a paper titled "Consequences of Erudite Vernacular Utilized Irrespective of Necessity: Problems with Using Long Words Needlessly" (get it?). When you use needlessly complex words, readers know, deep down, you are trying to show off.

Of course, we can't always be simple. When our ideas are complex or technical, we need to choose precision over simplicity. In philosophy, for example, we might not have any choice but to talk about ontology or epistemology; in religion, eschatology or Manicheanism; in physics, quarks and the r-process. So some ideas require complex vocabulary. But even complex words can be rendered simple. When you define a complex term clearly, with step-by-step explanations, analogies, and examples—*presto!*—the term becomes simple.

To get a sense of how prominent writers select and use words, look at this showing the percentage of complex words, the number of syllables per word, the number of words per sentence, and two measures of grade-level difficulty, the Flesh-Kincaid Index and the Fogg Index.

Author, Title	Complex words	Syllables per word	Words per sentence	Flesh-Kincaid index	Fogg index
Ernest Hemingway, *The Old Man and the Sea*	3%	1.3	14.4	4.7	7.0
Jeannette Walls, *The Glass Castle*	6%	1.4	15.8	7.2	9.2
Ken Follett, *The Pillars of the Earth*	8%	1.4	12.4	6.1	8.3
Truman Capote, *In Cold Blood*	10%	1.5	14.5	7.9	9.8
E.B. White, *Essays of E.B. White*	11%	1.5	20.9	10.4	12.6
Jon Krakauer, *Into the Wild*	12%	1.6	18.9	10.1	12.6

Richard Feynman, *Six Easy Pieces*	13%	1.5	21.2	10.8	13.8
Martin Luther King, *Why We Can't Wait*	14%	1.6	12.4	8.2	10.7
William F. Buckley, *Nearer My God*	15%	1.6	20.5	11.3	14.0
Stephen Hawking, *A Brief History of Time*	16%	1.6	15.2	13.1	16.3

Good writers vary in the complexity of vocabulary and sentence structure. There is no right or wrong percentage. Hemingway's words worked for Hemingway; Hawkings's words worked for Hawking. Some concepts require a greater range than others. But Strunk and White's basic truth—use what you need, nothing more and nothing less—holds here.

Language constantly evolves. We turn nouns into verbs and verbs into nouns. The process happens slowly, usually as conversational shorthand. Just think of all the nouns we now use as verbs: *contact, parent, author, impact, party, friend,* and *IM.* This is nothing new. Verbs like *rain, thunder, snow, show, audition,* and *critique* all started as nouns. Turning nouns into verbs usually makes expression simpler. After a period of confusion, these new uses gain traction.

But going the other way, from verbs to nouns—known as nominalizations—often makes language more complex. Consider the simple sentence: "President Obama made an announcement about health-care reform." *Announcement* is the nominalization. The problem is threefold:

- We create a noun that is hard to visualize. We can't see *announcement* as clearly as other nouns, like *senior citizen* or *table* or even *voice* or *touch*. As much as possible, we need to keep our language vivid, sensual. *Announcement* is clunky, even bureaucratic.

- We leave important points out. By turning a verb into a noun, you beg the question. President Obama made an announcement about health care? What did he say? When we keep the verb active, we are more likely to complete the thought. Like this: "President Obama announced that health exchanges increased enrollment by…"

- We strip the sentence of its lively verb. Always—always, always, always—strive to describe things with action. When you use nominalizations, you tend to use limp verbs like *made, had*, and *was*.

When in doubt, use the verb. Verbs shake, rattle, and roll—and keep the reader's attention. Nominalizations? Not so much.

....

#DENSITY

....

When you express complex ideas,
don't bunch together difficult concepts.
Give the reader some "space" to
absorb ideas, one at a time.

Art uses different kinds of space. Visual art—painting, illustration, photography, and graphics—uses the limited area of a canvas or paper. Music uses the "space" of time; each moment holds a new sound, which joins with other moments to create a complete work. Cinema combines the moment-by-moment experience of music with the visual experience of art, motion photography, sculpture and dance use three-dimensional space, one in fixed form and the other in movement.

Like music, writing creates a moment-by-moment experience, and each moment contributes to a larger whole. Each sentence and paragraph reveals something new. Even though you cannot view the piece as a whole, as you behold a great piece of visual art, you can hold all of the pieces in your mind. The more compelling the piece's composition, the more your mind's image of the piece holds together— and also the more you can appreciate its details.

The concept of density helps us understand just how writers fill their space. In architecture, density refers how many buildings and people fill a given space. A city like New York is packed with people and buildings; a city like Des Moines has a more open feel. The denser a community, the greater its complexity—and the harder it is to understand.

Dense writing—writing with lots of different ideas packed into a small space—also provides a complex environment. The problem is that that dense expression is often too hard to understand. Dense writing usually occurs in scientific and other specialized topics. Writing in science, for example, usually has greater density than writing about politics or relationships. Sentences carry more "content" words, that is, specialized terms. In their study *Writing Science*, M.A.K. Halliday and J.R. Martin show us the density of a number of sentences. (The content words are italicized; density scores follow the sentences.)

a. But we never did anything very much in *science* in our *school*. 2.

b. My *father* used to *tell* me about a *singer* in his *village*. 4.

c. A *parallelogram* is a *four-sided figure* with its *opposite sides parallel*. 6.

d. The *atomic nucleus absorbs* and *emits energy* in *quanta*, or *discrete units*. 8.

e. *Griffith's energy balance approach* to *strength and fracture* also *suggested* the *importance* of *surface chemistry* in the *mechanical behavior* of *brittle materials.* 13.

We read the first few sentences easily. The later sentences come hard. If we know only six of the eight content words in sentence (d), we might reach the end without any real understanding. Even if we know all of those eight terms, we might still struggle. Packing so many technical words so close together makes it hard to relate the ideas.

Writers rely on two ways to reduce density. One is to use more ordinary words. You might say "gives" instead of "emits" in (d), for example. But sometimes you need those technical terms. Then, the only answer is to break sentences into pieces. In (e), we can talk about Griffith's approach in one or two sentences, then talk about brittle materials, then mechanical behavior, then the effects of surface chemistry on behavior. Usually, we can break complex sentences into manageable pieces.

Whenever you need to explain a complex concept, remember this idea: *Good is great.* All great writing— or music, dance, visual art, or any other kind of expression—is really a collection of *good* pieces. All dense ideas can be broken down into less intimidating pieces.

Part 3

Structure

I remember the first time I visited the Eiffel Tower in Paris. The view from the top was amazing. In one direction you can see the Somme, in another the forest of Hallatte, in another the Chateau Thierry, in another the Palace of Versailles and the chapel of Dreux, and in another the forest of Lyons. The view has changed over the years. You now see more development—towns and housing complexes and parks and highways—but the wonder of the panoramic views still stuns. And of course, the tower is visible for miles. From 56 miles away, you can see the light at the top.

But for me, the greatest view comes from below. The first time I visited, I stood at the basic of the tower, leaning back to view the whole structure. It was dizzying. First I noticed the semicircle at the base of the structure. Then I looked at both ends of the structure and saw two lines rising from the ground, finally meeting almost 1,000 feet up in the air. Then I looked more closely at the actual structure of the pieces and saw endless, interlocking triangles.

After getting lost in the triangles, I started to notice the crisscross of lines, both vertical and horizontal, that held the triangles. Three basic shapes—lines, triangles, and circles—created this vast monument that has captured the imaginations of people all over the world since it opened in 1889.

I want you to think of the structure of your writing like the structure of a great monument like the Eiffel Tower. Consider how a collection of pieces—arcs and lines, circles and triangles—come together to create a coherent whole. Such simple shapes combine to create the most elegant and durable structures. Let's see how.

....
#LINER NOTES
....

Most outlines don't work because they tie you to a scheme that often turn out to be wrong. But flexible line outlines work guide your research and writing well.

Writing about the challenges of architecture, Stuart Brand once remarked: "All building are predictions. All predictions are wrong."

The same goes for outlines. So let's get rid of them.

From the time we first write "serious" papers in school, teachers insist the we use outlines. They usually look like this:

I. Major sections marked with Roman numerals
    A. Subsections marked with capital letters
        1. Parts of those subsections noted with Arabic numbers

              a. Details marked off with lower-
              case letters

The outline, we are told, offers a complete roadmap for our work; that roadmap makes writing easy. "If your outline is good, your paper should be easy to write," advises one university writing program. "Making a detailed outline before you begin writing is a good way to make sure your ideas come across in a clear and logical order," another university guide says. "A good outline will also save you time in the revision process, reducing the possibility that your ideas will need to be rearranged once you've written them."

Balderdash. Too often, outlines make writing a nasty mess. Rather than guiding the writing process down a clear path, outlines drive us into blind alleys.

The reason is simple. Outlines are predictions. At the beginning of the writing process, you don't really know what you want to write. You need to explore different ideas. You need to try different ways of expressing your thoughts. You need to abandon some ideas that seemed sensible at the beginning—and add new ideas that you did not imagine at the beginning.

Writing to an outline prevents you from doing the most important job of writing—*thinking*. Ultimately, it leads to confusion.

Sure, I know, you can adjust your outline as you go. You can treat your outline as a "first cut." You can add this line and delete that line. But that's hard. An outline, subconsciously, feels like a contract. Also, the outline's stair-step structure requires you to think hierarchically. But most ideas don't require such a detailed hierarchy. Most ideas—especially if you follow the "Paragraph Bucket" approach—are quite simple.

Also, outlines prevent you from thinking through your ideas. Standard outlines don't use complete sentences; they use disconnected phrases, concepts, notes, allusions, and numbers, which often don't mean much. So just when you think you're ready to write, you have to go back and figure out what you meant in the first place.

Still, it helps sometimes to use some sort of structure to organize writing. I suggest using "liner notes."

As you investigate your topic, write down the propositions that seem true. Write those propositions in boldface type. Do not worry about organizing these propositions in the right order.

As you gather information that supports these propositions, list that information under the lines. Use bullets to separate the ideas. Write this supporting information in light type.

Use complete sentences for all of these lines. Do not use telegraphic phrases. Express complete thoughts, with clear subjects and verbs. Do not worry about the quality of those sentences. You can fix that later.

After you write a dozen lines, consider organizing them into two or three groups.

Do not—I repeat, *do not*—create a stair-step format. Keep your propositions as simple and clear as possible. The moment you break propositions into multiple parts, you lose your clarity. You get lost in the weeds of your thought.

So what do "liner notes" look like? Take a look at some of the propositions I listed for a report I wrote about the future of manufacturing in New York City. These lines explore the 3D printing industry:

> The 3DP sector promises to transform manufacturing--from prototyping to real-time, custom manufacturing.
>
> > The 3DP sector is already experiencing growing pains.
> >
> > New developments in materials promise to make 3DP even more powerful.

When I wrote these liner notes, I had no idea how I would organize my report. I just knew that I needed to understand these basic propositions—the points I might want to make—and then to support these propositions with evidence.

After writing a couple dozen lines, I start to add supporting information. Here's how I might flesh out the first proposition:

The 3D printing industry promises to transform manufacturing—from prototyping to real-time, custom manufacturing.

- Before moving into mass production, companies can produce prototypes in a fraction of the time.
- 3D printing offers manufacturers a means to iterate the design of objects, so they can test those parts and adjust the design until they get it right.
- 3D printing offers an efficient means to meet small-batch demands for unique products.
- Rather than wait for a distant factory to produce an object, customers can get that object 3D-printed locally and delivered within hours.

As I worked on this report, I added, deleted, and combined some of the propositions. I moved the them around, until I found the right sequence. The liner notes allowed me to see the big picture, adjust my ideas, and fill in details when I found them.

Let's eliminate the tedious, clunky, over-stylized outline that we learned in school. Let's focus on what matters—identifying the major propositions that we want to express, expressing them fully, and gathering the evidence we need to support them.

....

#**SHAPES**

....

*Think about what kind of shape you want
to give your piece. Make the arc your
default shape. But also consider straight
lines, circles, and triangles.*

Once you identify all the points you want to make, give
them some shape.

The most important shape in all writing is the arc.
The arc takes the reader on a complete journey, with
growing intrigue and excitement, which concludes in
an emotionally satisfying way. Hat tip to Aristotle for
explaining the power of the arc, 2,500 years ago.

But you may wish to use other shapes to structure
your writing. Sometimes, after all, the reader does not
need the emotional engagement that the arc delivers.
Choose from three other shapes: The line, the circle, and
the triangle.

When you use a straight line, you assume that the
accumulation of events or arguments is what matters.
When you use a circle, you focus on the repetition of patterns. When you use a triangle, you assume that a steady
relationship among the three corners is most important. When you list four or more things, you assume that
something is too complex to simplify.

Let's see how by looking at Milan Kundera's classic novel *The Unbearable Lightness of Being*. The story

tracks three main characters—Tomas, a Lothario doctor in Czechoslovakia in the late 1960s; Tereza, the woman he meets at a spa and eventually marries; and Sabina, his on-and-off lover. Each is tested by the others—and by Communist system and Prague Spring revolution of 1968.

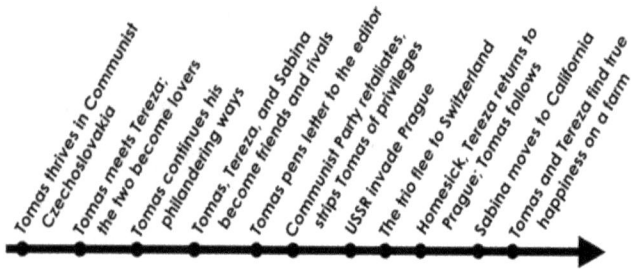

In the straight line, we see a simple sequence of events. The playboy doctor benefits from his elite profession to make a comfortable (if shallow) life for himself. He beds many women, including Sabina. At a spa, he meets Tereza, who soon shows up at his apartment. They become lovers, but Tomas continues his philandering ways. The three flee Prague during the Soviet invasion. Tomas and Tereza eventually return, while Sabina moves to California. Tomas and Tereza find happiness living on a farm. They die in a car crash after an evening celebrating with friends.

Kundera chooses to structure his story as a series of circles, as he hints in the novel's first paragraph:

The idea of eternal return is a mysterious one, and Nietzsche has often perplexed other philosophers with it: to think that everything recurs as we once experienced it, and that the recurrence itself recurs ad infinitum! What does this mad myth signify?"

We see the characters go through the same story, over and over. Each telling explores a different aspect of the story—lightness and weight, soul and body, words misunderstood, soul and body (again), lightness and weight (again), and the march forward. Each cycle offers fresh details that propel the story forward.

In each circle, Tomas flees something. Every time Tomas flees, though, he is forced to confront some new, deeper truth. Over time, as the same patterns repeat themselves, Tomas comes to a deeper understanding of himself and life.

Tomas, enjoying his fame and fortune, ignores his ex-wife and son. Then he meets Tereza.

Theme: Flight from responsibility.

To avoid the pain of hurting her, Tomas marries Tereza but still has a wandering eye ... and holds tight to his privilege.

Theme: Flight from honesty.

Tomas, stubborn and prideful, locks Czech authorities and loses his privilege. He leaves the country, but returns with Tereza.

Theme: Flight from his past ... and then from his loneliness.

Tomas embraces a new, simpler, better life, still with Tereza, but maintains his carefree ways.

Theme: Flight from privilege and egoism that restricted his development.

Finally, we can see the story as a series of triangles. Most obviously, there is the lover's triangle of Tomas, Sabina, and Tereza.

Another triangle involves Tomas, the Communist government, and the people he sacrifices when he defies the government. Another triangle involves Communist Czechoslovakia, Switzerland, and the United States.

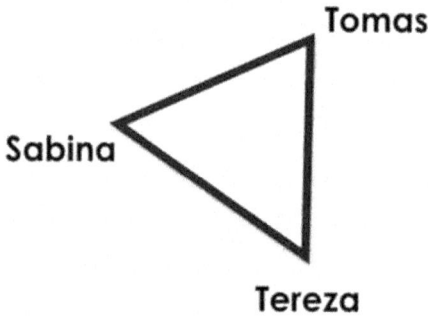

Tomas

Sabina

Tereza

The shapes of your writing—straight line, circle, or triangle—help to determine what you say. Content follows form.

#UNFOLDING

Avoid packing your ideas.
Let complex ideas unfold, one by one.

For the best example of how to explain it topic, turn to your cookbook. It doesn't matter which one you have. The Moosewood Cookbook is good. So are the works of

James Beard, Julia Child, and Paul Prudhomme. They all explain perfectly to carry out their instructions.

And how could it be otherwise? When you cook, you need to do everything in the right sequence. You can't chop vegetables after you cook them in a casserole. You can't crack and scramble the eggs after cooking the omelet. You can't pour the pie fillings into the pan before you've made the crust. In cooking, sequence matters.

So it should be with writing. Not all topics require a simple sequence of ideas. But many do. When you explain topics from the simple (how to set a splint) to the complex (how nuclear fission works) – it's best to unfurl a simple sequence of ideas.

Too often, however, we bunch up ideas. When we raise an issue, we cluster together a whole variety of related issues. We don't separate topics. We densely pack ideas, like sardines in a tin, rather than allowing them to present themselves, one after another.

The more complex your topic, the more important it is to take matters simply, one at a time.

Consider Kay Redfield Jamison memoir of suicide, *Night Falls Fast*. Jamison uses her own battle with depression, over many years, to explain just how uncontrollable an ill mind can be. In the following passage, Jamison describes the basic circuitry of the brain:

Everywhere in the snarl of tissue that is the brain, chemicals whip down fibers, tear across cell divides, and continue pell-mell on their Gordian rounds. One hundred billion individual nerve cells—each reaching out in turn to as many as 200,000 others—diverse, reverberate and converge into a webwork of staggering complexity. This three-pound thicket of gray, with its thousands of distinct cell types and estimated 100 trillion synapses, somehow pulls out order from chaos, lays down the shivery tracks of memory, gives rise to desire or terror, arranges for sleep, propels movement, imagines a symphony, or shapes a plan to annihilate itself.

Redfield focuses on only one aspect of the brain here— how chemicals zoom around the highways and byways of the brain. To do so, she zooms in on the brain's overall composition (e.g., "snarl of tissue," "three-pound thicket of gray," "shivery tracks of memory") and its infinitesimal components and processes ("one hundred billion individual nerve cells," "thousands of distinct cell types," "100 trillion synapses").

Step by patient step, Jamison sets up subsequent discussions of related matters. She can now explore how a person's genetic codes determine the brain's makeup, how environment shapes the brain's development, electrical communication inside the brain, how chemicals transit messages, how those transmitters fail, and how drugs affect communication. Later, she connects this "micro" analysis with the "macro" analysis of different regions of the brain and an even more "macro" analysis of a person's heritage and environment.

In a few pages dense with scientific terminology, Jamison gives us a picture of the brain at work. We can see what no naked eye can see. Jamison succeeds because she explores ideas one at a time.

By establishing a foundation, and then showing how things work, step by step, you can explain complex processes with clarity and verve.

....
#YO-YO
....

If you don't give your reader variety, you will get stuck in long and overwhelming passages. So yo-yo from long to short, specific to general, physical to cerebral.

"I hate a style, as I do a garden, that is wholly flat and regular," said William Shenstone, an English poet who was also one of the first landscape gardeners. "It slides along like an eel, and never rises to what one can call an inequality."

To see what he means—and why it matters for writing well—go to great Olmstead park or English garden. Or go to a museum to see a great landscape artist like

Pieter Brueghel or Nicholas Poussin, an impressionist like Monet or Renoir, or one of the painters in the Hudson River School.

Pay attention to patterns. What do you see?

Almost all the time, as the philosopher Denis Dutton informs us, you will see "alternating copses of trees and open spaces, often hilly land, with animals, water, and a path or river bank that winds into an inviting yet mysterious, bluish distance." When the landscape switches back and forth, from openness to density and back again, we feel at home. If all we saw was a vast open vista, or a dense cluster of trees or other growth, we would have a hard time understanding the scene's scope or context. We need both concentrations of nature and open space.

That is the lesson of yo-yo writing. The best writing moves back and forth, from the density of exposition to the openness of narrative. We need the packs of information that exposition gives us. But we also need the journey that stories give us. As Frank Sinatra crooned about love and marriage, you can't have one without the other.

Jack Hart outlines the two poles that good writers move back and forth:

Summary	Narrative
Emphasizes abstract ideas	Emphasizes concrete details
Collapses time, summarizing what happened into survey statements	Gives readers a minute-by-minute experience of what happens
Uses direct quotations	Uses dialogue
Follows a topical outline	Follows action, scene by scene
Uses an omniscient, distant point of view	Uses a specific person or group's point of view
Looks at the issue from a distance	Zooms into the middle of the scene
Focuses on causes and effects, with an emphasis on results	Lays out the process
Operates at the higher rungs on the "ladder of abstraction"	Operates on the lower rungs of the "ladder of abstraction"
Uses explication and backstory	Follows the story's movement over time, along an "arc" from the inciting incident to the climax

A masterpiece of yo-yo writing is Elizabeth Gilbert's "Lucky Jim," a profile of a man whose two serious accidents resulted first in amputation and then paraplegia. However much he has lost, Jim MacLaren has always found ways to give his life meaning. Every time MacLaren faced a major crisis—losing a leg, losing the use of his whole body, getting addicted to cocaine—he deepened his explorations of life's existential questions. Gilbert's story alternates, every two or three paragraphs, from Jim's action-packed life to his rumination on the meaning of that life.

I once coded Gilbert's piece. I put a red dot by every word that evoked the three senses—kinesthetic, visual, and auditory. When I finished, I found clusters of red dots throughout the piece, alternating with dot-free passages that summarized and explained issues.

For three or four paragraphs, Gilbert would use vivid description. Gilbert would describe the story's hero, Jim MacLaren, in action—riding a bike, training for marathons, getting in crashes, abusing drugs, raging against God, snuggling with his girlfriend. These paragraphs of rich description alternate with expository paragraphs—ruminations, background information, other non-action stuff. The back and forth works. She awakens the reader's senses, but doesn't overdo it.

See how Gilbert shifts back and forth from scene to summary. First look at her action scenes:

Jim MacLaren doesn't have any memory of the first accident. He can't tell you what it feels like to be hit by a New York City bus and thrown 89 feet in the air, to have your bones shattered and your legs crushed, to be pronounced dead on arrival at the hospital.

[Years later,] participating in a triathlon, he was speeding through the town of Mission Viejo on his bicycle at 35 m.p.h., leading a pack of cyclists past cheering spectators. Suddenly, Jim heard the crowd gasp. He turned his head to see what was going on, and there was the steel grille of a black van heading straight toward him. The racecourse had been closed to traffic except at certain intersections, guarded by the police. But somehow a van had been let through.

This time Jim vividly remembers being hit. He remembers the screams from the crowd. He remembers his body flying across the street and smashing into a lamppost head first, snapping his neck. He remembers riding in the ambulance, aware that he could not feel his limbs.

Now see how Gilbert steps back, away from action, and summaries the issues that MacLaren faces:

Jim is what's known as an incomplete quadriplegic. Although all four limbs were damaged when he broke his neck, he still had limited nerve activity, allowing him some movement and sensation. He can raise his arms a bit, bend forward in his wheelchair, use his hands somewhat, and sometimes even lift his legs by a few degrees.

This tiny range of movement means the difference between an independent life and one with round-the-clock caretakers. With excruciating effort, Jim can breathe, dress, and feed himself, and even drive a van (specially outfitted with only hand controls). This all came as a big surprise to Jim's doctors, who initially thought he would never have any feeling or motion below the point of injury. "So I've been very lucky," Jim told me.

There is a galvanizing momentum to recovery, but there eventually comes a wall where healing stops and the truth of what you're left with settles in. Jim had just hit that wall. His body had healed as much as it was going to. And all the determination in the world could not change the facts that he'd never be out of pain again, he'd never lift his arms above his head again, and he'd never walk again.

Most writing requires both narrative and explanatory passages. The scientific paper may not require the full narrative of MacLaren's story. And McLaren story doesn't need the latest research findings from academic journals. But to understand the whole piece, we need both approaches. We need to yo-yo back and forth from scene to summary.

Novelists used to place a narrator in the middle of a story and, at crucial stages, have the narrator turn to the reader to explain what was happening. Woody Allen sometimes does the same. In a witty BBC production called "To Play the King," the dastardly prime minister (nicknamed "F.U."), occasionally turns away from the action to address the camera.

That's what yo-yoing does. It moves back and forth from the story to the analysis.

....
#NUMBERS
....

To create focus and order in your
writing, organize events and ideas
by ones, twos, and threes.

Sometimes it takes a simple game and a modest man to explain what really matters.

And what matters for developing talent — in sports, musical instruments, acting, scientific research, business, and of course writing — is breaking down skills into the simplest pieces.

It's as easy as 1-2-3, as the winning coach of the

Little League World Series explained to me many years ago.

Back in 2005 I went to the Little League World Series to write a book on the changing world of youth sports in America. That year's winners came from Ewa Beach, a working-class community in Hawaii.

The team was assembled for the expressed purpose of winning the LLWS. Nothing else mattered. Rather than just cobble together teams for the sheer fun of play, a truck driver for the U.S. Postal Service named Layton Aliviado set out to build a team of superstars. Aliviado and his players actually created their own Little League organization to go for the glory of the Little League World Series. When they gathered at their practice fields they moved from station to station, working on vertical leaps, running through ladders, sprinting, fielding grounders, catching line drives, lunging, duck-walking, and doing long jumps. They moved fast, from post to post . . . and then started over again.

Aliviado taught the kids pitching, hitting, throwing, and running, with a simple 1-2-3 breakdown of the skills. When I visited Aliviado in his home, he grabbed a bat to demonstrate how he taught hitting: *set, shift, hit.* He narrated his movements.

"One: stride forward.

"Two: get the hips going, get the hands going.

"Three: bring the hands around into the zone, snap everything forward."

The key, he said, was to put everything in threes.

"In the beginning of the season, I do 1-2-3 drills," he said. "I keep it simple for the kids. Everyone can count. Just count out what to do and explain by showing. Then they have it stuck in their heads: 1-2-3. I do the same thing with throwing and pitching. Every kid can count, right?"

Writing has its own 1-2-3 code. So let's look how to use ones, twos, and threes to organize writing—and keep it simple.

ONE: When you name only one thing, you single it out for attention. One might be the loneliest number, as the song by Three Dog Night says, but it's also the most powerful number. When you name only one thing, the rest of the world fades into the background.

History books are filled with stories of singular characters—Caesar, Christ, Washington, Lincoln, Gandhi, King—who stand like a colossus in a world of little people. We can understand a lot by looking at such great men. But that focus can blind us to the complexity of the world. When we show how these giants are shaped by their complex environment, they tell a better picture.

Singular events also fill the history books. The Declaration of Independence, Gettysburg, the Great Crash, D-Day, Hiroshima, JFK's assassination, 9/11— these moments create a dividing line between before and after that simplifies the endless flow of events. After, 9/11, we said "the world is changed." And maybe it was, in some ways. But even though these days deserve attention, what we really need to know is what complex people and events made them happen. If we single out people and events for such analysis, we can understand the world in powerful ways.

Two: With twos, you can show how the battles of rivals. You can also show how people or things complement each other. Muhammad Ali and Joe Frazier, while fighting for the heavyweight championship of the world, also battled for each other's respect. John Kennedy and Richard Nixon, longtime colleagues in Congress, battled for the presidency; even after Kennedy's death, Nixon shadowboxed with Kennedy's ghost. Bill and Hillary Clinton, partners in life and power, battled with each other behind the scenes over policy and personal affairs, but defied all the tabloid predictions of divorce. Jeff Jeffries and Lisa Fremont, lovers in *Rear Window*, come from different worlds but grow closer while solving a murder mystery.

Two characters rarely sustain drama, though. With two characters, Robert McKee says, you get "not dilemma but vacillation between the positive an negative." It's a tug of war, in which one side will inevitably win. "With two characters, we see some drama, with characters pushing against each other. Both sides have to decide whether they love each other, hate each other, or don't much care. It's positive, negative, or neutral. But once that question is settled, not much remains."

THREE: Groups of three offer greater potential for plumbing the complexities of characters and issues. To Martin Scorcese, the director of classics like *Taxi Driver* and *Raging Bull*, the ideal scene "puts three people in a room." Why? Robert McKee explains:

> Triangles are dynamic. Everything a character does with another character also affects the third—and the balance of power among all three. Triangles reveal the weaknesses of people, which create tensions for all three people—and also offer the opportunity for change, good or bad.

Consider the great triangles of literature—Oedipus, Laius, Jocasta (Sophocles's *Oedipus Rex*); Mr. Darcy, Jane, and Elizabeth (just one of many triangles in Jane Austin's *Pride and Prejudice*); Santiago, the boy, and the disdainful townspeople (Hemingway's *The Old Man and the Sea*). Or consider triangles from movies and TV: Rick, Ilsa, and Victor (*Casablanca*); Julius, Paula, and Stefan (*Men*); Danny, Theresa, and Rose (*Only the Lonely*); Carrie, Mr. Big, and Aiden (*Sex and the City*). Finally, politics. Can you imagine a system of government with two, or four, branches? I can't. The executive, legislative, and judicial branches seem a perfectly tense balance for democratic rule.

Triangles offer a good approach to many abstract issues as well. All political battles, E.E. Schattschneider wrote in a classic book called *The Semisovereign People*, begin with two combatants. Unless one side defeats the other right away, the battle gets resolved with the entry of outside forces:

> Consider a conflict between A and B – inevitably changes the conflict. The entry of a third party, C, may join and tip the balance of forces in his favor, or he may support B and turn the other way. Or he may disrupt the conflict and attempt to impose his own resolution. No matter what he does, however, C will alter the conflict by transforming a one-to-one contest into a triangular drama.

Katherine Boo, a writer for *The New Yorker*, says the best arguments contain three distinct angles. "[T]hree well-articulated, nuanced examples—backed by sharply documented evidence of a broader problem—are far better than twenty examples that raise more questions than they answer," she says. "Stories that run in one, two or three parts, not sixteen, are more effective."

I bet movie-goers of the 1970s and 1980s can remember the first three "Rocky" films. But can they remember all six? Doubtful. The series lost its shape by the time it concluded three decades after the original.

FOUR OR MORE: Lists of four or more things gives priority to none of them. As a result, we have a hard time deciding what really matters. Consider, for example, the groups that Hillary Clinton would need to win the 2016 presidential election: Blacks and Hispanics, college students and other first-time voters, educated and whites, soccer moms and office-park dads, high-tech business interests, environmentalists, churchgoers, feminists, disgruntled Republicans, and maybe even supporters of the Green and Libertarian parties. Did I leave anyone out?

Long lists, alas, do not foster sharp analyses. You might as well say Clinton needed lots of votes from lots of groups. But of course! You could make the same point about Donald Trump, her Republican opponent, too. That's what a democracy is all about—getting more votes than the other guy. Which brings us back to smaller numbers. We would do better to focus on the three groups who could tip either way, and not pay as much attention to the others.

Whether you want to tell a story or make an argument, three looks like a magic number. It provides enough material for a compelling way to explore the world—whether it's the relationships of Ike, Tracy, and Mary in Woody Allen's *Manhattan* or the relationship between the executive, legislative, and judicial branches in American government—while not overloading the reader's circuits.

Part 4

Style

To understand style and the creative process, let me introduce you to a singer/songwriter named Valerie Orth.

Valerie writes songs that bend, break, and unite the standard categories of music. Some songs carry a pop flavor. I can imagine her single "Uh Oh" climbing the Top Forty charts. Other songs have a rapper's edge, sound folky, or take on a ska vibe. Some of her music has a Country Western feel and some has the darkness of a suspense film's score.

Actually, all of her songs contain all of these elements, in different combinations. She blends these styles together, in her own way, to express a range of ideas and feelings. How does she do it? Partly, it's a mystery. Her songs, after all, come out of her unique life as an artist. But a lot is not so mysterious.

First of all, Valerie works hard to build her music, line by line. Every morning, for example, she does 10 minutes of Object Writing. She takes an object—a hairbrush or a shirt or a book or a guitar or anything else that catches her attention—and writes about it. She forces herself to describe the object with six senses.

Valerie brings this attentiveness, this deep concentration to her work, every day. Deliberately, consciously, she writes her songs. She scribbles notes, edits them, sings, plays the guitar, and joins friends and partners to make the music together. She adds here, cuts there, bends here, trims there. Her music-making is a deliberate, conscious process of construction.

At the same time, Valerie lets loose. When she rides her bike from Brooklyn to Greenwich Village, she listens to her iPod or soaks in the sounds of the city. She tracks her dreams, keeping a pad of paper by her bed just in case. When she works on music-making software, she lets loose and allows herself to make mistakes that might—*just might*—contain a kernel of musical expression. Or, when teaching inner-city kids how to make music, she gets lost in their world. Who knows what she might find?

With these activities, Valerie Orth is creating a style that's all her own. She works hard, deliberately, paying close attention to the structure and grammar of musical ideas. But she also allows herself to gets lost in her everyday experiences. Without any specific goal, she makes sure that she experiences the parts of life that she cannot predict ahead of time.

To find your own style as a writer, follow Valerie's example. Concentrate and work hard on the fundamentals. But also let loose, forget about the rules, to discover senses and ideas. Move back and forth, from discipline to looseness. Then put the pieces together, in your own way.

....

#SENSE AND SENSIBILITY

....

> *Reading is a sensual experience.*
> *So use the senses to connect with*
> *the reader's physicality.*

Consider the following questions:

You are in a store, checking out backpacks. You are looking for a leather one. How do you go about checking whether the item is made of leather or man-made materials?

You are riding in a cab. A nostalgic, sad song is playing, followed by one with an upbeat rhythm and a sexual pulse. How would the music affect your mood?

When you are in an art gallery, in what manner do you look at the paintings?

Do you enjoy petting furry animals (allergies aside)?

You are given a bouquet of flowers. Your first reaction would be…

You are a completely alone on a private island and there is a crystal-clear lake. It's hot and you could use a swim. You …

You have set out to furnish your living room. What would best describe the type of furniture that you choose?

How do you feel about things like the smell of a spring breeze, the air shortly after rain, a brisk winter wind, the ocean, or a sunny day?

How often do you engage in meditation or deep breathing exercises?

When walking down the beach, do you take off your shoes or sandals?

When you read a novel, do you picture the scenes in your head as you're reading them?

These questions are part of a sensuality test that *Psychology Today* posts on its website. (Take it yourself at http://bit.do/sensualitytest.) The test helps you to understand just how *physically* you experience the world with your senses of sight, sound, touch, and smell.

My purpose here is to get you to write physically. Even when exploring dry and abstract topics, I want you to think sensually. When you do, you can connect with your reader—capture her attention, hold it, get it to consider your ideas wholeheartedly, and remember and reflect what you want to convey.

Language, I submit, is a physical experience. When you use language well, you can make your audience connect with the topic physically. A description of cold creates a shiver; of music, a sense of rhythm and time's pacing and feel; of texture, a tactile feeling of smoothness or roughness or slipperiness or more; of light or shapes, a sense of appearance.

Whatever you write, think consciously about the physical words you use.

SIGHT: What do we see when we see? We see brightness, color, shapes, texture, and proportions. We see relationships between things.

Often, when I am working on research or a draft, I need to visualize what I'm thinking before I understand it. So I draw pictures—shapes showing relationships, levels of importance, movement, and more.

If you can get your reader to see your subject, you have won the battle. It's as if you're side by side, looking at a painting in a museum, like Edward Hopper's "Nighthawks." *See those lonely people in the diner? It's late. Nothing's happening outside. Everyone looks so alone. But the couple—they're together, right? Are they on a date or just getting a smack after a long night at work. They don't look intimate. The soda jerk is paying attention, though. What about that man at the end of the diner? He's really alone.* Once you start to see the pictures, you start to tell the story—and interpret what it means.

Also give your writing color. The colors' many qualities—primary or secondary, dark or bright, simple or complex—contribute to a mood. In music, color describes a piece's emotional feel. Beethoven's Fifth Symphony evokes darkness, while his Fourth evokes brightness.

Colors also conjure emotions. Red evokes power and sexuality, yellow intelligence and joy, blue tranquility and patience but also coldness and depression, orange courage and confidence, endurance and friendliness, and green money and nature.

FEELING: In three-dimensional art, texture refers to how a piece actually feels when touched. Henry Moore's bulbous, polished sculpture, at Kew, England, look and feel smooth. Rodin's uneven and pock-marked clay surfaces, like the "Gates of Hell," feels rough. In one-dimensional art like painting and photography, texture refers to how it *looks* like the piece would feel; texture in music and writing involves how a piece *sounds* like it would feel.

In writing, evoke texture by evoking the sounds that we hear when encountering physical things. Hard consonants sound rough and sharp, while soft consonants sound smooth. The word *crackling* sounds rough, while *luminescent* and *slither* sound smooth.

SOUND: Take a moment, right now, and listen intently for a minute or more. What do you hear? The drone of the dishwasher? The rattling of the wind on the window panes? The stentorian voice of the announcer on TV? The murmur of neighbors outside on the sidewalk? The laughter of children in the yard? The song of birds in the tree? The almost silent sound of the cat walking across the floor?

Sounds tell us not just about the subject but also about the mood. Sound—*even just words about sound*—makes us pause, lean in, and listen. Sound makes us attentive. Think of the times in your life when you stopped doing something … because … you *heard* something. "What's that?" you asked. You could not continue until you learned something about the sound. You needed to find out whether it mattered.

The power of language is really the power of sound. Alliteration—the repetition of the same consonant sounds—somehow evokes meaning. S's sometimes sound slithery, sometimes soft, and sometimes hissing. K's sound hard and abrupt, almost like a collision or an attack. L's sound lilting and lithesome, light and uplifting. P's sounds somewhat silly, plopping and plunking and puffing along. We could go on.

Don't think too hard. Just listen to the sounds you write and pay attention to how they make you feel. You'll know when there's a fit and when there's not. Now look at these images:

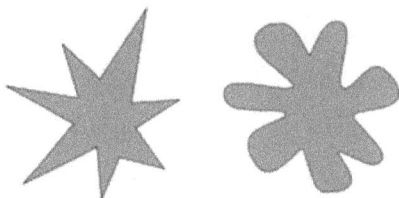

Quick! Which one is the *booba* and which is the *kiki*? I'll bet that you say the shape with the round, bulbous edges was the booba and the one with the spikes was the kiki. It just seems obvious, doesn't it?

Trust your own feelings here. Pay attention to what you hear and what it makes you think and feel.

The biggest challenge of sensual writing is getting the "fit" right. Readers get confused and stuck when the senses you evoke don't match the ideas or feelings you describe. You can't describe someone's soft touch with hard sounding words. You can describe someone's intelligence with dark or bright words, but they suggest different kinds of smarts.

The purpose of sensual writing is to connect with the reader—use universal feelings and sensations to express something.

#PICTURES

Think in storyboards—or, if it's more
convenient, in PowerPoint slides.

To most people, grammar is an ugly stew of abstractions—parts of speech, verb tenses, irregular forms, complex syntax, and irregular spellings.

Enter Eugene Schwartz, a legend in the field of advertising. To Schwartz, traditional grammar is a big, ugly barrier to clear writing. In his classic book *Brilliance Breakthrough*, Schwartz writes:

> If you were taught grammar in school, your
> ability to speak well, and write well, was

crippled. … You have to realize that there are no such things as nouns, pronouns, verbs, adjectives, and all the rest. … None of them show you how to take your thoughts, put them into words, and link the words together into sentences that are simple, that are clear, and that make other people think the way you do.

So what does Schwartz propose as an alternative? Pictures. Good writing, he says, should be like going to the movies. The best writing presents a series of pictures. Those pictures convey the full human experience—emotions and ideas, hope and fear, problems and possibilities, concepts and conundrums.

Consider the following sentences:

Martin Luther King linked arms with his followers to defy the police on the bridge to Selma, Alabama.

Tom Brady took the snap, stepped back, surveyed the field, and uncorked a perfect spiral to Julian Edelman.

After sifting the flour and beating the eggs, my grandmother poured the ingredients into a bowl.

Each sentence offers clear, distinct pictures. We can (to take the first example) *see* King, the locked arms, the line of followers, the police, and the bridge. Each word-picture activates our brain's vast database of images. Then we put those images together to create a picture, show-ing clear, vivid action.

Pictures words convey not only physical things, like people and places, actions and events, sequences and conflicts. They also convey concepts. Let's play a game. Tell me the picture that you see when I state the follow-ing ideas:

Strength

Freedom

Ego

Opportunity

Future

Difficult

Democracy

Every one of those words conjures up images. When you hear *freedom*, you might picture people working, voting, relaxing, or avoiding unpleasant tasks. Or you might conjure up a symbol of that idea—like the Liberty Bell in Philadelphia or the Statue of Liberty in New York. When you hear *ego*, you might picture someone with confidence—someone strong and serene and com-petent. Or you might picture ego gone awry, a boastful braggart or a bully. Whatever you picture, you picture *something*.

Whatever you write, make sure to give the reader visuals. Show the reader what things look like—their size and scale, their shapes and colors, their textures and lights, their speed and sounds.

Whenever you decide to write something, sketch it out before hand—and throughout the process—as a series of simple images.

Once you have considered what images tell your story—or explain your process or make your argument—you need to connect those images. So use connecting words like *a, them, in, over, and, yet, to, when*, and *before* (to name just a few) to relate the pictures to each other. These words do not show the reader anything. But they prepare the reader for pictures and they relate the pictures to each other.

Thinking in pictures is easy. We do it all the time. But when you're writing, it takes some effort. Before putting your fingers on the keyboard, you need to pause, maybe even close your eyes, and slow down the rush of your ideas. Picture by picture, you can then translate those ideas into clear, vivid prose.

....
#THIS AND THAT
....

Remember the fundamental rule of all understanding: To know one thing, you need to compare it to something else.

We cannot know the world directly. I cannot look at, say, a tree and know what it is. I need to understand the tree with knowledge of related concepts—nature and ecosystem, plants and growth, trunks and branches and leaves, dirt and water and oxygen. I can only know a tree by understanding other concepts. And so, when I write, I need to make comparisons of my subjects with related (and sometimes unrelated) things.

Metaphors state that one thing is another thing, even though, logically, that could not be so. X cannot be Y, not literally anyway. But pretending allows us to see some Y-like qualities in X.

Metaphors work by surprising and orienting the reader at the same time. We are surprised by the connection between dissimilar things, but oriented by how we start to see something familiar in something unfamiliar. Shakespeare said, for example, that "all the world's a stage." Of course, the world isn't a stage, with scripted lines, a limited number of characters, a time limit for action, exotic costuming of the way the characters break out in song or poetry or slick witticisms. But in a larger sense, the world is indeed a stage. We constantly present ourselves to others—acting—to convey our own ideas or stories. We give defined roles to ourselves and others. So, yes, the world *is* a stage!

Politics, usually the most conventional of businesses, sparkles with metaphors. Malcolm X, who sharpened his rhetorical blades on the street corners of New York, dismissed the potential for a nonviolent revolution in civil rights by comparing Mohandas Gandhi in India and Martin Luther King in the United States: "Gandhi was a big dark elephant sitting on a little white mouse. King was a little black mouse sitting on top of a big white elephant."

Malcolm rejected the call for racial integration with an appeal to blackness:

> It's just like when you've got some coffee that's too black, which means it's too strong. What you do? You integrate it with cream; you make it weak. If you pour too much cream in, you won't even know you ever had coffee. It used to be hot, it becomes cool. It used to be strong, it becomes weak. It used to wake you up, now it'll put you to sleep.

Malcolm rejected the movement's talk of love and redemption. To make his case, he needed to offer a different perspective.

If metaphor equates one thing with something different, its cousin, the simile, takes a more casual approach. "Metaphors are forceful," say former Poet Laureate Ted Kooser and his collaborator Steve Cox. "Similes are, like, casual." The metaphor says X=Y; the simile says X≈Y.

You could say the savannah is *like* a carpet, teeth are *like* Chiclets, a voice is *like* a foghorn—or that the ballplayer is as brave *as* a warrior, the smile as bright *as* the sun, or the student dumb *as* an ox. My favorite comes from James Thurber, the *New Yorker* humorist who wrote "The Secret Life of Walter Mitty." Speaking of his memory, he told *The Paris Review*: "It's … well … like a whore's top drawer. There's so much else in there that's junk—costume jewelry, unnecessary telephone numbers whose exchanges no longer exist."

Similes exaggerate. To say the smile is bright as the sun, is so false that even discussing would be absurd. Scientists tell us that the sun's luminosity is the equivalent of 4 trillion trillion—that's 4,000,000,000,000,000,000—100-watt light bulbs. On a sunny day, you cannot look directing into the sun, which is 93 billion miles away. Surely, no smile is that bright. So, it's an exaggeration. But such an exaggeration makes a point, doesn't it?

Still, a good simile can help you see the world in fresh ways. Thomas Lynch, describing a cadaver in a body bag, writes: "Wrapped in white plastic top to toe, and—because of his skinny head, wide shoulders, ponderous belly, and skinny legs, and the training white binding cord from his ankles and toe tag—he looks, for all the world, like a larger than life-size sperm." Comparing a cadaver to sperm sounds disrespectful, but Lynch's goal is to unsettle old assumptions and inject humor into a grim business.

David Sedaris notices the discomfort of nudists in clothes; they appear, he says, "ornery and uncomfortable, like cats stuffed into little outfits for the sake of a wacky photograph." I like this simile because it tells us the opposite of what we might think. Being undressed is like being dressed. When you reverse roles—people undressed, pets dressed—you offer a fresh perspective on oddness.

Wilfred Sheed describes Jackie Robinson's daring base running: "He ran the bases like a kid with a switchblade, so that when he got caught in a rundown one felt sorry for the infielders." Everyone knows of Robinson's grace under the trials of racism when he broke major league baseball's color line. But to truly understand Robinson's character, you have to understand the toughness behind that grace. Sheed captures Robinson's daring with the image of the one instrument Robinson would never carry.

Finally, Anne Lamott describes the lingering pain from childbirth: "The wound feels like there's a fishing weight suspended from its highest point; the weight swings like a pendulum and drags the wound downward." As painful as that image is for me, it's probably more painful—and more real—for women who have given birth. It has the same *ouch* effect as the zipper scene in *There's Something About Mary*. If a simile can make you respond physically, it works well.

Each simile works because each evokes a clear image, making us see a small piece of reality in new ways.

> *Once you have mastered simple*
> *and direct communication, give your*
> *writing some tempo and color.*

Two kinds of mindsets prevail among writers.

The Clear and Simple School, insists that the purpose of writing is to inform and entertain as simply as possible. Partisans of this style call for short sentences, simple words, and uncomplicated messages. Forget about symbolism or erudite allusions. The Clear and Simple School is the literary version of Joe Friday: Just the facts, ma'am.

The Rococo School, insists that clear and simple is really shallow and boring. Why not jazz up the prose? Why not create several layers of meaning, even in the simplest phrases? Why not offer the reader new discoveries with every reading of a piece?

In fact, the two schools are not as incompatible as they might seem. You see, even the most ornate prose is usually just a collection of simple phrases and ideas. When you break down a master of literary riffing, like Tom Wolfe or Hunter S. Thompson, you see a string of simplicity.

Consider this 122-word sentence from William Faulkner's *Absolom, Absolom*:

From a little after two o'clock until almost
sundown of the long still hot weary dead
September afternoon they sat in what Miss
Coldfield still called the office because her father
had called it that–a dim hot airless room with
the blinds all closed and fastened for forty-
three summers because when she was a girl
someone had believed that light and moving air
carried heat and that dark was always cooler,
and which (as the sun shone fuller and fuller
on that side of the house) became latticed
with yellow slashes full of dust motes which
Quentin thought of as being flecks of the dead
old dried paint itself blown inward from the
scaling blinds as wind might have blown them.

Now look at this passage, idea by simple idea:

From a little after two o'clock
until almost sundown
of the long still hot weary dead September
afternoon
they sat
in what Miss Coldfield still called the office
because her father had called it that
–a dim hot airless room
with the blinds all closed
and fastened for forty-three summers

> because when she was a girl
> someone had believed that light and moving air
> carried heat
> and that dark was always cooler,
> and which
> (as the sun shone fuller and fuller on that side of
> the house)
> became latticed
> with yellow slashes full of dust motes
> which Quentin thought of as being flecks
> of the dead old dried paint
> itself blown inward from the scaling blinds
> as wind might have blown them.

Faulkner, you see, is a poet—or maybe he's a pointillist painter. He dabs dots of color and light onto his canvas, accumulating details, until he has produced a complete portrait that you can see in one viewing.

So why did Faulkner press all of these ideas together as one thought? I think he wanted to capture how we experience the world as a rush of ideas and sensations. If he had broken up the passage into two or three or four sentences, readers would pause before moving from one to the next. But gathered together in one all-encompassing thought, the passage brings these ideas together into one moment, the way a river brings together its tributaries into one grand rush of water.

When you want to pepper your prose with style,

don't think you need to be elaborate. In fact, think the opposite — that you need to be as simple as possible. If you find the specific details that others might not notice — and then bring these details together — you will wow the reader — then you'll wow the reader.

Let me leave you with one warning, though. *Don't overdo it.* Audiences love to be dazzled. They love the energy and the color of passages like this. But they can get overwhelmed too. Alternate this kind of linguistic pyrotechnics with a simpler, shorter style. Then you'll have the best of both simplicity and complexity.

#IDIOMS AND MEMES

To speak to your audience, take on at least some of the style of your audience.

Consider this simple thought:

> Every community wilt lay-to a corse of sooths
> and quillets, rendering ideas gross in sense.
> To receive each other, we need to wot our
> common proof. Not to be tetchy, but let's
> agnize that varlots resort to long-engraffed
> bootless, whoreson saws and other mooncalfs
> that still slubber things. Want-wits use these
> thought-executing waftages mostly in prate.

Got it? Anyone in the English-speaking world should understand this simple passage. Anyone, that is, from Elizabethan times. Audiences at the Globe Theater would have understood these words from Shakespeare's plays, not only the literal meanings, but also the values and images they evoked.

All communication requires a store of common ideas and words. The more vocabulary the reader and writer share, the easier the communication. We need to use familiar words and expressions, questions and ideas, to make a connection. But at the same time, we need to make sure we don't deaden the conversation with old clichés that do not mean or evoke much.

Good writers tap into the common knowledge of their civilization. Writers need to understand the Declaration of Independence, Shakespeare, the opening theme of Beethoven's Fifth, $E=mc^2$, DNA, the old brain/new brain dichotomy, "Dewey Defeats Truman," the Gettysburg Address, Confucius, bits and bytes, *The Peloponnesian War*, and countless of other reference points of world civilization.

When you refer to an important cultural concept, you often point to a cluster of meanings. Consider the closing lines of Abraham Lincoln's first inaugural address:

> We are not enemies, but friends. We must not
> be enemies. Though passion may have strained

> it must not break our bonds of affection. The
> mystic chords of memory, stretching from
> every battlefield and patriot grave to every
> living heart and hearthstone all over this
> broad land, will yet swell the chorus of the
> Union, when again touched, as surely they
> will be, by the better angels of our nature.

The idea of the "better angels of our nature" has become iconic. The phrase evokes people's mix of good and bad tendencies. But it also evokes Lincoln himself, the tragic war he fought, his generous attitude toward enemies, and the optimism and hope that animated his life. Even out of context, the passage would touch us. But for people who know Lincoln, the layers of meaning provide even more power and subtlety.

Some of the most powerful idioms and memes come from mythology, the Bible, and literature. These stories touch us deeply because they speak to timeless values and dilemmas.

Joseph Campbell's *The Hero With a Thousand Faces* outlines a "meta-narrative" that captures the essence of every conceivable tale:

> A hero ventures forth from the world of
> common day into a region of supernatural
> wonder: fabulous forces are there encountered
> and a decisive victory is won: the hero comes

back from this mysterious adventure with the power to bestow boons on his fellow man.

Think of all the great stories that follow this arc of departure, initiation, and return—*The Odyssey. Paradise Lost. Zen and the Art of Motorcycle Maintenance.* The journeys of Jesus, Buddha, and Muhammad. The tales of King Arthur and the Roundtable. Moses leading his people out of Egypt. Beowolf. "Joseph and His Technicolor Dreamcoat." *The Straight Story*.

The Bible offers timeless ideas for storytelling. The parables of Jesus—the stories of the mustard seed, the thief in the night, the laborers in the vineyard, the good Samaritan, and the arrogant guest, to name a handful—vibrate in our common heritage. Consider the parable of the prodigal son. A young man takes his inheritance early, leaves his father's farm, falls into a life of degeneracy, and then returns home to his father's loving embrace. This tale teaches eternal lessons about the arrogance of youth, the anger of the dutiful brother, the need to learn through experience, and the abiding love of family.

Timeless tales and ideas provide touchstones that resonate with people. Tap into this culture, and you can connect with people at all levels of their being.

#CLICHES

To give clichés life—to make them fresh and original again—find something surprising to add to them.

Too often, we use familiar ideas without really understanding their meaning. We repeat phrases and ideas carelessly.

When we overuse expressions, we live in a *fool's paradise*. We *cannot hold a candle* to the *halcyon days*, our *salad days*, when we *suited the action to the word* and revealed *the naked truth*. But we *give short shrift* to language, writing with *neither rhyme nor reason*. And we lose *such stuff as dreams were made of*. That's *neither here nor there*, since these expressions are *dead as a doornail*. *Coming full circle,* we realize, *more in sorrow than anger*, and it's *a foregone conclusion* that overuse of such terms is a *fatal vision*. So, *in one fell swoop*, we *throw cold water on it*.

All of those expressions come from Shakespeare. These expressions once expressed ideas with freshness and originality. But used over and over, they have lost their vitality. Too often, we use these clichés not because they express ideas well, but because they offer a simple way to say something. They let us say something without thinking.

Remember you want to make the reader see, feel,

smell, taste, touch, imagine—and *think*. The more familiar the images, the less you will engage your reader.

"Cliches," Geoffrey Hill notes, "invite you not to think." Cliches give use easy, lazy was of expressing ourselves. As Hill notes, "you may always decline the invitation." When you feel tempted to use a cliché, stop. Get in the habit of considering how to state a point simply—or think of a fresh, original way of making a point.

To avoid the dreariness of clichés, play with them. Start by looking at its literal meaning. Porter Abbott explains:

> When the orator urges his or her auditors
> "to strike while the iron is hot," how many of
> them see the sweating blacksmith at his forge
> and feel his magical transmutation into new
> meaning? The answer is none. … But when
> one tramp suggests to another that "it might
> be better to strike the iron before it freezes" the
> original vehicle is revived in its literal state.

Taking words literally reveals the cliché's original insight. When you do a genealogy of clichés, you discover vibrant images that can be revived.

When you change the context of cliché, you can give it new life. In a memoir of his life as an undertaker, Thomas Lynch writes about the death of a neighbor: "Milo is dead. X's on his eyes, lights out, curtains.

Helpless, harmless. Milo's dead." By using the slack, disinterested tone of a gumshoe, Lynch moves us away from sickly sentimentality.

Samuel Beckett uses clichés in playful ways to make them fresh. He writes: "Personally I have no bone to pick with graveyards." And then, describing the odor of graveyards, he added that he will breathe in the smell of corpses "when take the air I *must*." In her memoir of family suicide, Joan Wickersham freshens a stale image: "Cal may have had pots of family money, but my husband didn't even have a small saucepan."

Whenever possible, though, avoid clichés. Lush detail—observation of sights, sounds, smells—helps to create original expressions.

Nack could just say, "I thought about that horse day and night. I couldn't get Secretariat out of my mind. It popped up no matter where I was or what I was doing" *Zzzzzz*. Instead, Nack uses compelling images to show how Secretariat shaped every minute of his life.

Write like Bill Nack. Always look for the fresh images—ideas that are familiar, but which other writers have not used before—to help the reader experience the scene.

....

#DETAILS

....

To engage readers, show them details.
Notice the things that most people miss.
Look intently at every scene. First take
in what's obvious. Then probe for
what's not so obvious—which
could be even more important.

You know about Abraham Lincoln. Since childhood, you have heard the storybook legends—his childhood poverty, the death of his mother, his thirst for learning, reading by candlelight, traveling down the Mississippi, his strength and humor, his life as a lawyer, the Lincoln-Douglas debates, a term in Congress, election as president, a troubled marriage, presiding over the Civil War, and assassination at Ford's Theater.

So if someone wants to tell you about Lincoln, you want something fresh. You don't want to hear haggard stories and clichés. Now, how about the following passage?

> He then greeted us all round, not waiting for
> an introduction, but shaking and squeezing
> everybody's hand with the utmost cordiality,
> whether the individual's name was announced to
> him or not. His manner towards us was wholly
> without pretense, but yet had a kind of natural

dignity, quite sufficient to keep the forwardest of us from clapping him on the shoulder and asking him for a story. A mutual acquaintance being established, our leader took the whip out of its case, and began to read the address of presentation. ...[H]e jerked or wiggled himself out of the dilemma with an uncouth dexterity that was entirely in character. ... The gist of the reply was that he accepted the whip as an emblem of peace, not punishment; and, this great affair over, we retired out of the presence in high good-humor,

Nathaniel Hawthorne's description of meeting President Lincoln—who skillfully deals with his visitors' strange gift of a whip—tells us something about the man. We see Lincoln as both clumsy and graceful, simple and grand, casual and respectful. By using specific details—about the people, occasion, place, gift, remarks, and reaction—Hawthorne offers a scene that remains fresh almost a century and a half later.

"The true enemy of man," Czeslaw Milosz says, "is generalization." We can only understand a subject when we make the effort to observe details. When we pay attention—to faces and body language, the words and sounds of everyday life, the shapes of buildings and things—we begin to understand its basic character and its complexity.

So how do you offer such fresh and surprising

details? *Wherever you go and whatever you do, take lush notes.* Look for the details that would surprise or inform even a well-informed reader. A rich collection of details give you the opportunity to pick just the right one, rather than one that sort-of, kind-of works.

Incorporate details into your writing in two ways. The first way is to freeze time to paint a portrait of a person, place, or process. After setting up a situation, you zoom in on a character and stop the action, as if hitting the "pause" button on a video player. Then describe the person, her looks and sounds, posture and bearing.

Thomas Lynch offers this freeze-frame description of the casket of two six-year-olds who died falling through the ice of a river: "We put them in one casket with two pillows, foot to foot—identical in their new Oshkosh B'Gosh jeans and plaid shirts their mother had mail-ordered from Sears for Christmas."

The second way to show details is to describe a scene, with movement, as Scott Russell Sanders does in his memoir of growing up with an alcoholic father:

> In the perennial present of memory, I slip into the garage or barn to see my father tipping back the flat green bottles of wine, the brown cylinders of whiskey, the cans of beer disguised on paper bags. His Adam's apple bobs, the liquid gurgles, he wipes the sandy-haired back of a hand over his lips, and then his bloodshot gaze bumping into me, he

stashes the bottle or can inside his jacket, under
the workbench, between two bales of hay, and
we both pretend the moment has not occurred.

If details give writing energy, adjectives and adverbs
deplete that energy. Adjectives and adverbs are linguistic bullies. They tell readers what to think, rather than
offering information for the readers to assess.

Sometimes, you need an adjective to explain an
image. Sanders writes: "You swallow the bitter quinine
of knowledge, and you learn to feel pity and compassion
toward the drinker." When Sanders uses the word "bitter" to modify quinine—a drug extracted from the bark
of a South American tree—he helps us to understand an
obscure allusion. If he used something more familiar,
like a lemon, talking about its bitterness would fail.

Part 5

Cleaning up

The trouble began when Mother left Sally and her brother home on a bleak, rainy day. When the kids heard a bump at the door, they met a playful feline ready to have some fun. In walked a tall, slightly mad cat wearing a hat and a bowtie. Then the chaos began.

You probably know the story of the Cat in the Hat, the most famous character from Dr. Seuss' children's stories. The cat's arrival brings fun and games. When the pet fish objects, the cat balances him on the tip of an umbrella. Then he holds a whole set of household items—books, a toy boat, milk, and a cake—until he loses his balance and everything falls to the floor.

Soon the Cat in the Hat introduces his miniature friends, Thing One and Thing Two. The Things fly a kite, knock pictures off the wall, and play with Mother's polka-dotted nightgown. Mother's house is a mess when the children spot Mother returning home. What to do?

Not to worry, announces the id-like cat. He leaves the room, then returns riding a giant machine. Nine hands extend from the machine to clean the house. The machine's hands pick up objects, sweep, dust, and make the house as neat and clean as it was before. Even the persnickety fish is tickled by the cat's playful cleanup game.

We writers are the kids and the fish. When we write, we create a mess. Even when we try to keep things organized, our inner cat makes a mess. Meanwhile, our inner fish frets and worries. If only we could drive in a big cleanup machine, like the Cat in the Hat, to clean it all up.

I can offer no such machine. But I can offer a simple approach to cleaning up your drafts.

For many writers, editing is a distasteful part of the writing process. We love playing with words and ideas, but cleaning up afterwards is a thankless chore. But of course, editing is the key to all good writing. As Francine Prose says, "All writing is editing." Or as Ernest Hemingway says, "Write with your heart, edit with your mind."

....
#**EDITING**
....

Editing requires noting the things
that we missed first time around.
To overcome "familiarity blindness,"
use some simple tricks.

Some pieces of writing require an overhaul. Tinkering on the edges will not fix much. We need to tear down the structure, sort the materials, throw some away, add a few more, and use a new blueprint.

IDENTIFY THE SECTIONS: The key to writing about complex topics, according Malcolm Gladwell, the pop-ideas writer for *The New Yorker*, is to divide a long argument or story into a number of mini-essays.

Any long piece should really be a series of separate pieces, each with its own question and answer. Gladwell advises limiting those sections to 1,200 words. That's about five or six double-spaced pages. Why 1,200 words? Most people need a break. We lose focus when we push ourselves too hard, both mentally and physically. So give the reader moments to pause, to absorb ideas and mentally prepare for the next passage.

Why do most movies fizzle after two hours? Why do most pop songs last around three minutes? Why do most business meetings degenerate into repetitious back-and-forth after an hour? Why do children need to get up and move every half-hour or so?

When you write a long piece, make sure you understand the point of every paragraph—and the point of every section. Avoid filibustering the reader. Remember, the reader can put down your writing at any moment. The world holds lots of other diversions. To keep the reader with you, do not push too far.

BREAK PARAGRAPHS INTO IDEA BUCKETS: As noted elsewhere, every paragraph should express one clear idea. You should be able to label a paragraph with a two- or five-word phrase that captures its essence.

If a paragraph contains more than one idea, break that paragraph into pieces. State each idea clearly, then provide the information you need to develop it. If one of those ideas does not contribute much to the essay, cut it. Take out every paragraph, sentence, and word that does not contribute to the piece's major point.

IDENTIFY THE S-V-O CORE: Build every sentence around a strong subject, verb, and object. Cut everything that does not strengthen that S-V-O core.

Read this passage from "The Other Side of Hate," by Andrew Corsello:

> Jim Steele was mad as hell. His blacks were messing with the farm, and the land was always personal. He'd been born on the farm. Like many Rhodesians, his parents had planted his umbilical cord in the ground so the boy's life and the good earth would nourish each other forever. This land held the blood of his dead brother, his soul mate, thirteen months younger, who at age nineteen had reached into the truck for the shotgun and accidentally tripped its hammers, taking both barrels in the stomach and crying "My God!" as he fell. The blood of my brother in the ground. Though Steele called himself a Christian, the earth itself was his real religion and his good and proper use of it, a form of

worship. Any abuse of the earth or the fruit it brought forth was an assault on his person.

Take that paragraph and mark the subjects, verbs, and objects. Then stand back and see how that simple core idea—S-V-O—allows the development of larger, more complex and subtle, ideas.

This paragraph offers a model of simplicity. We never lose track of what's happening: *Jim was mad. Workers messed around. Land matters to Jim. Land symbolically contains new and old life. Land is spiritual.* Of course, Corsello says much more than these telegraphic thoughts. He tells us his story will be tragic. He signals that the story concerns the deepest ideas of identity and memory. He shows us how the land deals with birth and death. He suggests some troubling ideas—for example, the simple phrase "his blacks" suggests that blacks belong to Steele as property—that he will need to resolve in the essay.

Only with a strong structure—S-V-O—can Corsello develop those subtler, more complex ideas. Simplicity makes complexity possible. So before you do anything else, make sure you get the simple things right.

LOOK FOR REPETITION AND NEEDLESS WORDS: Most early drafts are full of repetition, meandering, and clumsy phrasing. Finding the right way to say something takes time and effort. When writing, the creative juices get flowing—sometimes too much. As you think about an idea, you tend to repeat yourself. You wander off the subject. One idea reminds you of something, so you write about that; that reminds you of something else, so you write about that. Before you know it, you have wandered far off the topic.

Too often, writers repeat ideas by using just slightly different words for the same thing—redundant pairs. So teachers tell us to "compare and contrast." Or politicians tell us they will care for "each and every" voter. Or business executives tell us that "first and foremost," we have to cut costs. Each of these pairs says the same thing twice.

We also use needless adjectives and adverbs. Ever hear a commercial offering a "free gift" for opening a bank account? We also hear people talk about future plans, end results, armed gunmen, unconfirmed rumors, living survivors, past history, actual experience, real experience, advanced planning, and natural instincts. Each of those expressions repeats a simple idea.

Beware, also, the Ted Baxter Disease, the tendency to use pompous phrases to seem more important. You remember Ted, the egotistical anchorman on the old "*Mary Tyler Moore Show*." To cloak his inferiority, he used words he could not even pronounce. "Insofar as" and "To the contrary notwithstanding" and "attached find herein" are some of the most common office examples. But watch out, also, for fat words like *cognizant* and *facilitate* and *transpire*.

Finally, consider the problem of hedges and emphatics. Hedges happen when the writer lacks confidence. A hedge tells a reader, in effect, "I'm not really sure what I'm going to tell you." Hedges include words like *almost, virtually, perhaps, maybe, usually, somewhat, and sometimes*. Words like that pretend to modify a point, but give the reader little real information. Writers use them to avoid getting to the heart of the matter.

Emphatics use blanket statements to push the reader. "As everyone knows" is a classic emphatic. So are *of course, naturally, understandable, interestingly,* and *surprisingly*.

People use emphatics to stress a point, even if that extra stress is not needed. People use emphatics in conversation to counter others' ideas. So "he's not creative" gets the rejoinder "Actually, I would say he's in fact *very* creative." You could just say: "He is too." Somehow, that does not seem adequate. But it is. It is almost always enough. (Get it?)

TRANSFORM BIG PHRASES INTO SMALL PHRASES:

Writing is a lot like mining. To get the nuggets of gold, we have to excavate all kinds of other rocks and minerals. Once we get the gold, we need to get rid of the detritus.

Often, simple ideas get lost in long phrases. Consider this sentence from a government memo: "In order to facilitate the planning and preparation for the new fiscal-year budget, the Mayor and his staff members should assess the performance of different programs and line items to determine which achieved their objectives in the most efficient manner possible in today's public-opinion client." Stated more simply: "City Hall needs to find out what programs work best before preparing a new budget."

LOOK FOR PREPOSITIONAL PHRASES: Too often, writers string together phrases like lights around a Christmas tree. Prepositions connect those phrases, keeping the sentence going and going. A preposition, recall, connects nouns, pronouns and phrases to other parts of a sentence. The most common ten prepositions—*of, to, in, for, on, with, at, from, by,* and *out*—are among the thirty-seven most frequently used words in the English language.* If you fail to watch out for them, they will take your writing onto long detours.

Consider this example from *The New York Times*: "U.S. Secretary of State Condoleezza Rice *on* Monday dismissed Iran's response *to* a proposed solution *on* Tehran's nuclear program *in* Geneva *over* the weekend *as* 'small talk' meant to buy time."

Those strings of phrases force the reader to trudge

---

* *Other prepositions to that hijack your sentences are: about, above, across, after, against, along, among, around, at, before, behind, below, beneath, beside, between, beyond, but, despite, down, during, except, in, inside, into, like, near, off, onto, outside, over, past, since, through, throughout, till, toward, under, underneath, until, up, upon, within, and without.*

down a long path to find the treasure. The point here is that Rice dismissed Iran's diplomatic move on nuclear technology. Try this: "Secretary of State Rice rejected Iran's approach for ending the nuclear power crisis."

Often, the prepositional phrases do not really concern the main topic. These word clusters tempt the writer to wander off subject. We do not have to work very hard to imagine an addendum to the *Times* passage—"during a period *of* testing *as* the war *on* terrorism *in* the United Nations" and so on.

The worst offender is *of*. This two-letter word acts like a cancer, metastasizing throughout sentences and paragraphs and killing any hope of clarity. Begin your editing process by searching for every *of* in your draft. Cut the phrases that do not add meaning. Then look for other propositional phrases. Repeat. That alone will sharpen your prose immeasurably. Then look at the remaining prepositional phrases. Some provide useful information but still need work. You can blend many ideas from prepositional phrases into strong nouns. Consider this passage:

"Martin Luther King preached for a movement with nonviolent tactics; he argued that winning the battle of public relations would help to with legislative battles with moderate whites."

Blending the ideas from three prepositional phrases produces this strong passage:

"Martin Luther King embraced nonviolence to

transform American society. To get Congress to abolish Jim Crow, he said, required rallying moderate whites."

That editing required recasting the whole passage. When we eliminate strings of prepositions, we can find stronger ways to express ideas.

READ BACKWARDS: By the time you begin editing, you know too much. When you know a piece too well, you do not pay attention to clumsy passages, repetitions, missing words, redundant ideas, and other problems. Somehow you need to break the spell. You get lost in the flow of the familiar.

The answer is to read backwards. Read the last paragraph first, then the penultimate paragraph, then the ultra-penultimate paragraph, and so on. You will be surprised at easily you see bad and repetitive writing.

READ ALOUD: All too often, in the age of print, we neglect to pay attention to how words flow when spoken aloud. When we read silently, we chunk words; we do not read each word, but instead recognize groups of words. But when we read aloud, we can spot the typos and clumsy, wordy or vague sentences. When you hear the words, you can't hide anymore. Words on paper should flow well when they're stated aloud.

When you first read aloud, you first notice how confusing long sentences can be. With a little work, you can chop long sentences into two or three shorter sentences—and, just as important, remove all the words that obstruct the flow of ideas.

Assume an announcer's voice, and read each sentence. If you stumble, you have found a place that needs revision. Now, use the tricks we have discussed to fix it. As the back of the shampoo container says: "Rinse. Repeat."

Pick up a great book—a classic—right now. Read something by Truman Capote or John McPhee or F. Scott Fitzgerald. Find the poetry of Wordsworth or Shakespeare or T.S. Eliot or e.e. cummings. Or get a well-edited magazine, like *The New Yorker* or *The Atlantic*. Read a passage aloud. Notice how the words glide—or, when they do not glide, how bumps make you pause—and why.

#PUNCTUATED

To guide your reader through your ideas, offer some sign along the journey so they know when to stop, pause, look ahead, merge, connect, and take notice.

Years ago, Victor Borge did a routine called "Phonetic Punctuation." To help people hear punctuation marks, he added distinctive sound for each one mark. The period was a popping sound. The dash was a zipper sound. A comma was a popping sound with a twist—kind of a short, popping dash. The question mark was a longer zipper sound within exaggerated turn. An exclamation mark is a dash with a period. And so on.

Borges was just doing a silly routine for Borscht Belt clubs. But you could read a serious point in Borges's corny routine. Punctuation changes the movement of a sentence.

Punctuation directs traffic. Punctuation tells the reader whether to stop (period), slow down (comma), pause (question mark), look forward (colon), yield (semicolon), or proceed with caution (ellipses).

Here's a more precise way to understand punctuation:

PERIODS: The period is the writer's best friend. By marking the end of the sentence, the period gives permission for another thought. Many writing problems can be solved with a liberal dose of periods. Most bad writing happens when the writer wanders off the subject. One thought reminds you of another, then another, then … Before you know it, you have wandered deep into a thicket with no way out.

The period offers the solution. Use a scythe to chop the sentence into pieces. Keep the parts that say something important. Make sure that each sentence has a subject and verb. Problem solved.

If you can learn to make a simple statement, and then stop, you will become a good writer. Mark Kramer, a former curator at the Nieman Foundation, used to hold out his cupped hands and say: "Here's an unlimited supply of periods. Use 'em all you want. No limits!" You could almost *see* those dots filling his hands, so dense they looked like caviar.

COMMAS: If good writing depends on flow, the comma is the writer's second-best friend after the period. Commas create pauses in the sentence, giving the reader a brief moment to sort out ideas.

Commas serve two technical functions. First, commas separate items in lists, so we do not get lost in a long train of nouns. So: "Willie Mays could hit, hit with power, catch, run, and throw."

Some editors say you can delete the last comma in lists. While commas separate the first four items, the word *and* separates the last two items. Not to get to tetchy, but I disagree. Without that last comma, "run and throw" sound like a single skill. Most people, of course, would understand running and throwing to be separate skills, especially with the use of *and*. But why risk even a brief flash of confusion?

This is the classic "The woods are lovely, dark, and deep" problem. Robert Frost's poem "Stopping By Woods on a Snowy Evening" contains that memorable line. The line means different things with and without that last comma. With the last comma, *lovely*, *dark*, and *deep* refer to three separate attributes of the woods.

Without the last comma, *dark and deep* tells us what Frost means by *lovely*.

Commas, like em-dashes, also act as parentheses. Therefore: "Willie Mays, a first-ballot Hall of Fame member, can claim the title as baseball's greatest living player."

COLON: When you look through the viewfinder of a camera, you narrow your perspective to something in front of you. The colon acts in much the same way. Colons offer a way to halt a sentence, momentarily, so you can see what lies head. The colon indicates that some kind of explanatory information or list follows.

This explanatory information takes two forms: a phrase or a list. A colon sets up some modifying phrase after a complete thought. So: "Before his election as president, Abraham Lincoln had the same experience as Barack Obama: eight years in the state legislature and two years in Congress." A colon also sets up a list. So: "Winter is coming, so get our your cold-weather gear: coats, hats, gloves, boots, and ear muffs."

SEMICOLON: This little bastard of a punctuation mark— as one critic calls it—performs two major tasks.

The first, and only mandatory, function of the semi-colon is to separate items in a complex list. The semi-colon groups items into separate pieces. In this case, the semicolon acts as a super comma. Therefore: "To win the presidency, Democrats need to win Northeastern states, like New York, New Jersey, and Connecticut; Rust Belt states, like Ohio and Illinois; and liberal bastions, like California, Oregon, and Massachusetts."

The semicolon's second function is optional. The semicolon creates a break—and a connection—between two complete thoughts in one sentence. So: "William Buckley was a polymath; he was a writer, editor, speaker, activist, harpsichordist, and sailor." We could express those thoughts in two sentences or use a comma to separate the thoughts. But the semicolon offers a middle ground. A semicolon causes us to pause longer than a comma, but not as long as a period.

Some people hate this odd-looking little symbol. Novelist Cormac McCarthy calls it "idiotic." Bill Walsh, a copy editor at *The Washington Post*, says, "The semicolon is an ugly bastard." Kurt Vonnegut called semicolons "transvestite hermaphrodites representing absolutely nothing." But I say: Sheesh, why such emotional reactions to a sideways wink? Why not allow an extra tool into your toolbox? Sometimes you want to express two related thoughts without the period's abrupt, severe break.

HYPHENATION: If a German were in control of the English language, he would create a host of new words by combining several small words. Das Sprachchef would start by hyphenating those words. Inevitably, the hyphens would disappear and we'd end up with words like randybutbrainypoliticians to describe people like Bill Clinton and Elliot Spitzer.

That day has not come, and so we rely on hyphens, small dashes that look like -, to combine words into singular entities. Hyphens offer a great way to show how things relate to each other. Consider the following sentence: "East-coast liberals like Hillary Clinton differ from West-coast liberals like Jerry Brown." We could say "liberals from the west coast," but that's not as pithy.

Of course, connecting too many things with hyphenation can get silly. Like: "The first-term-African-American senator from south-side Chicago made his first-ever run for the White House in 2008."

EM-DASHES: If you want to set off whole phrases or lists like parentheses, turn to an elongated hyphen known as the em-dash. Look at this sentence: "The Chicago Cubs' inability to win a World Series for 100 years—a period that saw nineteen different presidents—has caused angst among their fans." Using the em-dash here gives the author the opportunity to make an aside. The em-dash tells the reader to pause, as if to say, "Hey, check *this* out."

I have been accused of being in love with the em-dash. A friend once told me that the em-dash is a cheap maneuver, which allows you to talk too informally, interjecting thoughts without much thought or care. But as Aristotle taught us, any good thing remains good in moderation. It's only when we overuse something—like this—that it becomes annoying.

ELLIPSIS: Every time I see an ellipsis—a set of three dots—I hear the sound of harp music that TV and movies use to suggest daydreaming. Ellipses (plural of ellipsis) suggests thought trailing off. Rather than bringing a lingering thought to an abrupt halt with the ever-decisive period, ellipses allow us to drift for a moment.

Consider the sentence: "Dorothy considered her challenge: 'If only I could see the Wizard of Oz . . .'" We see the girl with braided hair, a wicker-basket, and her dog Toto looking off into space, in her own world, wondering . . .

Suppose we could not group these dots together. Suppose we had to bring every sentence to a strong end. We would lose the ability to create a wistful or uncertain mood. We would, in other words, be taking away an important part of the human experience.

Ellipses perform one other technical task: They indicate gaps in quoted passages. When you quote someone, you often leave out whole sections of what they say. People rarely speak in compact packages; when writers quote people, they often need to stitch together comments made at different moments. To indicate that the words came at different times, use ellipses. Therefore:

"Ask not what your country can do for you—ask what you can do for your country. … Let us go forth to lead the land we love, asking His blessing and His help, but knowing that here on earth God's work must truly be our own."

PARENTHESIS: Sometimes, you want to turn away from the subject under discussion and offer a tidbit of related information. That information might strengthen the argument (providing details or context) or simply offer an aside (Ban Yagoda is one writer who loves parentheses).

Using parentheses too often can make writing choppy. But sometimes you want to show how choppy the world can be. "So are my parentheses part of my style?" Yagoda asks (rhetorically). "Actually, yes. I am drawn to them in part because they express my belief that the world and language are multifarious, knotty, and illuminated by digression."

Parenthesis also provide background information efficiently. Soon after Barack Obama was elected president in 2008, he began to build an administration from America's elite universities. Here's how *New York Times* columnist David Brooks described the emerging team:

Jan. 20, 2009, will be a historic day. Barack Obama (Columbia, Harvard Law) will take the oath of office as his wife, Michelle (Princeton,

Harvard Law), looks on proudly. Nearby, his foreign policy advisers will stand beaming, including perhaps Hillary Clinton (Wellesley, Yale Law), Jim Steinberg (Harvard, Yale Law) and Susan Rice (Stanford, Oxford D. Phil.). Here an elite, there an elite, everywhere an elite. Brooks makes this point nicely.

APOSTROPHES: This raised comma (') does two things. First, it shows possession. Therefore: "Clinton's impeachable crime was lying to investigators" and "The Clintons' allies rallied behind Hillary before the New Hampshire primary." The apostrophe also combines nouns and verbs in contractions. So: "Bill Clinton's a native of Arkansas."

QUOTATION MARKS: To indicate that you are using someone's exact words, use quotation marks. So: "Ask not what you country can do for you," President Kennedy said. "Ask what you can do for your country."

If you want to paraphrase, quote only the words that were spoken and use your own words to connect the phrases. After challenging the nation to "ask what you can do for your country," President Kennedy challenged other nations to "ask not what America will do for you, but what together we can do for the freedom of man."

If you want to connect the pieces of a passage, use ellipses (three consecutive dots). So: Kennedy challenged the American people: "We dare not forget today that we are the heirs of that first revolution. … Let every nation know, whether it wishes us well or ill, that we shall pay any price, bear any burden, meet any hardship, support any friend, oppose any foe, in order to assure the survival and the success of liberty."

Punctuation should almost always be put inside quotation marks. Therefore: "'Ask not what your country can do for you,' Kennedy said."

....
#**BARNACLES**
....

After writing a draft, go back and systematically eliminate all the unnecessary verbiage.

When I was a freshman in college, my English professor returned a paper with no marks besides a simple note:

Clear away the barnacles from your writing.

Barnacles are the marine creatures that attach to sea vessels of all sizes, from dinghies to aircraft carriers. Over time, barnacles create a kind of rough carpet that creates a drag on the boat. The harder you try to scrape them off, the more tenaciously they cling. The extra weight and drag can add increased fuel costs by 40 percent.

My professor was telling me, metaphorically, that my prose was bloated and slowed down with unnecessary verbiage. I was using many words when just a few would do the job. Specifically, I was:

- Setting up a discussion when I should just get to the point.
- Getting distracted, moving into discussions not germane to the topic.
- Repeating words, phrases, and ideas.
- Using meaningless adjectives and adverbs.
- Using emphatics and hedges, which pretend to support a point but don't.

Barnacles are inevitable. All of us tend to write the way we talk, with stops and starts, curves and trackbacks, digressions and repetitions. When we write, after all, we are exploring ideas. We play with language until we get the right words and phrases.

Happily, we can scrape off the barnacles from our prose. Here's how.

When you edit a draft, break it down into pieces. Identify the thought you wish to convey in each piece. Then start pruning. Eliminate the words that, inevitably, attach themselves to your writing. Scrape the barnacles off the boat of your prose.

Consider, for example, this passage:

All paragraphs are built on the first sentence,
and the following sentences in the paragraph
should run in a natural flow from it. Although
the paragraph is a flexible form, most readable
paragraphs depend upon connectors, sometimes
a word in one sentence that is repeated in
the next. The connectors tie your sentences
together-and therefore link your thoughts. You
can often test paragraph coherence by seeing
if every sentence has connectors that join its
thought in some way to the previous sentence
all the way back to the first sentence in the
paragraph. Similar patterns of repetition hold
all prose together. Each sentence both repeats
something from previous sentences-a word, a
synonym, or an idea-while adding something
new to the information readers already possess.

To be clear, that passage is not awful. I've read a lot worse. But I bet we could clear away the barnacles and make that vessel move more swiftly.

Start by identifying the basic ideas. Then figure out what action takes place. Then look for the barnacle words that stick to the main ideas and ask if they're really necessary. Here's how I would analyze and fix the passage:

The original	The idea	The revision
All paragraphs are built on the first sentence, and the following sentences in the paragraph should run in a natural flow from it.	Everything in a paragraph follows from the first sentence.	The first sentence anchors the paragraph; later sentences flow from the first.
Although the paragraph is a flexible form, most readable paragraphs depend upon connectors, sometimes a word in one sentence that is repeated in the next.	We need to connect the thoughts from one sentence to the next.	Paragraphs vary, but many use "connectors," including words that repeat from one sentence to the next.
The connectors tie your sentences together—and therefore link your thoughts.	Connectors relate your thoughts.	Connectors tie sentences together—and link thoughts.

You can often test paragraph coherence by seeing if every sentence has connectors that join its thought in some way to the previous sentence all the way back to the first sentence in the paragraph.	To assess a paragraph, see whether connectors create a logical chain of thoughts.	To test a paragraph, check whether connectors create a chain of ideas that support the paragraph's main idea.
Similar patterns of repetition hold all prose together.	All writing uses connectors.	All prose uses connectors to link ideas.
Each sentence both repeats something from previous sentences—a word, a synonym, or an idea— while adding something new to the information readers already possess.	Every sentence adds something new to something familiar.	Every new passage— whether a sentence, paragraph, or section— builds new ideas onto previously developed ideas.

Let's see what the new paragraph looks like:

> The first sentence anchors the paragraph; later sentences flow from the first. Paragraphs vary, but many use "connectors," including words that repeat from one sentence to the next. Connectors tie sentences together—and link thoughts. To test a paragraph, check whether connectors create a chain of ideas that support the paragraph's main idea. All prose uses connectors to link ideas. Every new passage—whether a sentence, paragraph, or section—builds new ideas onto previously developed ideas.

The revision cuts the number of words from 124 to 76. By removing the barnacles, you make the argument better and faster. With the extra space, you could add examples to illustrate your points. You might, for example, add a word of explanation about connector words. Or you could conclude the paragraph by reviving the opening idea—the first point leads to a chain of supporting points.

Oh, by the way, the passage comes from a book by Jacques Barzun called *Simple and Direct*.

....
#BARNACLES, PART DEUX
....

"Search and destroy"
four common problems that
create barnacles in your writing.

Of all twentieth century American writers, no one enjoys a reputation for brevity and clarity more than Raymond Carver. One critic called Carver "the quintessential minimalist, seemingly reducing to an absolute spareness both his subject matter and his treatment of it." Carver emphasizes brevity. "Get in, get out," he says. "Don't linger." His published work reflects that advice.

Except …

Carver's drafts were, at first, untamed and sprawling. His editor, Gordon Lish, often did the hard work of slimming down Carver's drafts into their terse, elegant final versions. Lish cut hundreds of words at a time, leaving behind the quiet, spare moments that won Carver acclaim.

You need to be your own Gordon Lish. Look for all the words and phrases that get in the way of your message.

Consider four common barnacles that encumber writing—and what you can do to fix them:

1. BUMPER WORDS: Too often, we warm up before getting to the point. We use words that say what doesn't need to be said. For example:

It is interesting to note that…
The fact that…
The reason why…
In order to…
In my opinion…
I have come to the conclusion that…
Currently…
At this point in time…

You can delete all of these words. You might say they're harmless, like clearing your throat before talking. But they use too much of the reader's attention. They require the reader to perform unnecessary tasks—deciding if these words matter or not. So avoid these unnecessary bumpers and get to the point—right away.

2. REDUNDANCY AND REPETITION: In conversation, we see how our audience responds—with nods and other signals of recognition or looks of confusion and incomprehension. In writing, we have no way of knowing whether the reader "gets" what we say. As a result, we have the tendency to rephrase and repeat what we say.

Don't.

If you say something clearly, you have no need to

say it again. In fact, saying it just once *emphasizes* the point.

3. LOST ANTECEDENTS: When you come into a conversation in the middle, you can't expect to know everything that's going on. So you interrupt: *Hold on—who said that? Who's she? When was that? I'm confused—was that before or after?*

But when you read something, you should never experience that confusion. The writer owes the reader total clarity.

Readers get most confused when they can't figure out the basic W's—who's doing what, when, where, and why. The problem is greatest when the reader has to track a number of people, events, and ideas. Consider, for example, the following passage:

> When Alexandra and Leila joined the crew,
> they knew they found their "inner circle" for
> life. Their friends from classes and clubs were
> important, but they couldn't compete. They
> offered a good balance with their sporting life. But
> that's where they got their deepest friendships.

This passage gets confusing. *They* first refers to Alexandra and Leila, then (twice) to their friends from classes and clubs. *That's* is also confusing. Does it refer to their other friends or rowing team?

So keep your antecedents clear. Whenever possible, place the pronoun closest to the word that it refers to. When necessary, provide the full reference so you don't confuse anyone. Here's how we might fix the above passage:

> When Alexandra and Leila joined the crew,
> they knew they found their "inner circle"
> for life. Friends from classes and clubs were
> important. But no one could match the
> friendships among the rowers. The non-rowers
> offered the girls balance. But the crew offered
> a chance for deep and enduring friendships.

4. NOMINALIZATIONS: Another common problem of our time is the nominalization—the use of a verb or adjective as a noun. So we talk about applicability, carelessness, difficulty, intensity, reaction and refusal. These words work well enough. But sometimes, nominalizations make us sloppy. Rather than using active words to describe actions ("The detective investigated the crime"), we use a limp nominalization ("The detective conducted an investigation of the crime"). The more we get away from active verbs, the less clear is our writing.

That's all. If I write any more, I'd just be adding barnacles to this discussion. And we're trying to avoid that, right?

Onward

....

#RELAX
....

You cannot succeed by putting pressure on yourself. We need to learn how to relax, so that we can focus intently on our work.

Most of our problems, not just when we write but also in other areas of life, are our own making.

The Buddhists, I think, have figured out the greatest problem of life. It's *attachment*. Whenever we become attached to something—objects, ideas, prejudices, memories, fears, fantasies, relationships, habits, routines, and so on—we suffer. When we tighten up, we get rigid. We lose sight of reality. We lose our ability to see and act clearly. We become critical of ourselves and others. We tie ourselves in knots. How, when so encumbered, could we act freely?

So far, in this short guide, we have not talked about the myth of writer's block. Do a Google search for *writers block* and you will get 4.24 million results. The first is this definition: "The condition of being unable to think of what to write or how to proceed with writing."

All writers have gotten stuck while trying to write. But I call writer's block a myth. Why?

Too often, we try to write with an overburdened, distracted, anxious mind. We try to force ourselves to write, before we're ready. When the words don't flow, we tighten up.

In my experience, the so-called writer's block stems from two basic factors:

- We have not done adequate research, so we try to describe or explain something before we have the essential information.
- We try to do too much, too soon. Rather than just taking it one line at a time, we try to write a whole section. Rather than laying out some simple markers—like the liner notes—we try to push through and write full paragraphs and sections before we're ready.

My advice—which, by the way, I sometimes do not follow myself—is to take it easy.

If you don't know what to say, do more research. Go to the library or the internet. Interview some more people. Draw pictures and charts of the ideas you want to explain. Express your ideas as liner notes—simple propositions that you can later explain in more detail.

Don't think about all the pressures of writing—deadlines, grades, contracts, lawsuits, popularity, sales, or anything else.

Just relax, take a deep breath, clear your mind and write …

One line …

After another.

The Dazzling Dozen

The best way to master writing is to study the masters. Here are twelve contemporary writers whose works merit your attention and imitation. Am I saying these are the *best*—or that I could ever make a list of bests? No way. I am saying, however, that each of these writers offers a distinctive lesson on the craft of writing.

Truman Capote, *In Cold Blood*: When a Kansas family was murdered in cold blood in 1959, Truman Capote decided to undertake an experiment that he called a "nonfiction novel." Using the techniques of the novelist, he would document the murder's impact on the rural town of Garden City. Capote lived in Garden City and visited for years, ultimately gathering 8,000 pages of notes. The result is a masterpiece of writing, with its powerful scenes and character development, yet clear point of view, artful yo-yoing from scene to summary, and flawless sentences and paragraphs.

Henry Roth, *Call It Sleep*: Possibly the best book on American immigration, *Call It Sleep* tells the story of a young Jewish boy growing up in early-twentieth-century New York. The novel shifts back and forth from the intimacy of the home to the rough-and-tumble of the street and school. Almost Joycean in its evocation of people and places and moods, *Call It Sleep*'s lush details and evocation of the senses creates a powerful drama involving David Schearl, his conflicted parents, his aunt and cousins, the boys on the street, the rabbi at his *cheder*, and strangers from dock workers to cops.

Laura Hillenbrand, *Unbroken* and *Seabiscuit*: Through diligent research, Laura Hillenbrand has been able to bring to life two long-lost legends: the unlikely thoroughbred champion Seabiscuit and the Olympic athlete and World War II prisoner of war Louis Zamperini. Every one of Hillenbrand's paragraphs rolls with specific, vivid, telling details about her subjects and the times and places that animated their spirits. Every paragraph is a story in itself, talking the reader from one specific state to another. Exciting but not overwhelming, these works reveal Hillenbrand as one of the greatest stylists of our time.

Jane Jacobs, *The Death and Life of Great American Cities*: While living in New York's Greenwich Village in the 1950s and 1960s, Jane Jacobs developed an anthropologist's understanding of how cities work that ran counter to the conventional wisdom of large-scale master planning. Her close observation of everyday activities in streets, sidewalks, parks, and buildings reveals a more organic understanding of urban life. Always modest in tone, Jacobs finds the details that are both familiar and surprising.

John McPhee: This *New Yorker* writer's oeuvre covers an astonishing spread—basketball, tennis, trucking, geology, nuclear proliferation, nature, Alaska, sea life, aircraft, teaching, and more. McPhee masters his complex subjects, explaining complex ideas simply, with metaphors that relate to common things and ideas. McPhee's longform works, whether magazine or book length, provides a strong of complete and satisfying paragraphs, which are combined to create complete and satisfying sections and, ultimately, a complete and satisfying whole piece.

Joan Didion, *Slouching Towards Bethlehem*: Irony and fatalism best characterize the essays, stories, and books of this quintessential voice of 1960s California. *Slouching Toward Bethlehem* is a masterpiece of observation and detachment. *The Year of Magical Thinking*, her memoir about the death of her husband, hovers on the edge of grief and analytic reserve. Didion's digressions offer peerless case studies on the art of blending rumination about past and present.

Joe Eszterhas, *Charlie Simpson's War*: If this book crackles like a fast-cutting movie, it should come as no surprise. After an early career as a narrative journalist,

Eszterhas became one of the most successful (and controversial) screenwriters of the late twentieth century. This work chronicles an American town rent by the cultural battles of the 1960s and 1970s, involving the Main Street establishment, liberal radicals, and blue-collar disaffected. Every scene crackles with vivid action, followed by simple and telling explanations of the larger changes taking place in society.

Ta-Nehisi Coates, *The Beautiful Struggle and Between the World and Me*: One of the greatest stylists today, Coates might be understood best as a writer of simple accumulation. He produces spare, right-branching sentences. After beginning (usually) with strong trunk—a clear subject and verb—his sentences spread like tree branches to explore the many aspects of the subject. One by one, these sentences accumulate to produce works of rare intensity and clarity. With this style, Coates writes unflinching analyses of the unceasing American dilemma of race. Even liberal allies contest some of Coates's claims. But everyone agrees that his mastery lays bare the dilemmas about race that we struggle mightily to conceal.

Karen Armstrong, *The History of God* and other works: For more than 30 years, Karen Armstrong has explored the simplicity and complexity of faith across the world. Her works make the familiar unfamiliar and the unfamiliar familiar. Somehow—by explaining, like a trusted friend—she avoids making religion preachy. By exploring religions on their own terms, she enters the lives and logic of believers. She takes her time, allowing the reader to absorb her lessons about Judaism, Christianity, Islam, Buddhism, and more. Over time, her patience gives her work the depth of a prayer.

Andre Agassi, *Open*: Tennis great Agassi tells a harrowing story of his personal battles with his father and the game that brought him fame and fortune. Agassi's rawness, honesty, and directness would make this a good book. But Agassi also has the rare quality of "negative capability," John Keats's term for the ability to hold contradictory ideas and feelings at the same time. Agassi hated tennis and he loved it; he hated fame and thrived on it. This book, ghostwritten by J.R. Moehringer, uses the present tense and eschews the use of direct quotations. The effect is a sense of immediacy as powerful as the last set of a championship game.

Elizabeth Gilbert, *Lucky Jim*: Liz Gilbert gained fame with her bestselling *Eat, Pray, Love* and *Committed*, which explore her search for herself through travel and marriage. But she was a master of narrative long before, with her works *The Last American Man* and *Pilgrims*. Nothing displays her skill better than "Lucky Jim," a tight profile of Jim MacLaren, a Yale grad who lost a leg when a bus hit him in New York and was then paralyzed when a truck hit him in the Hawaii Ironman event. MacLaren's journey took him from a typical understanding of the self as a body with mind and feelings to a deeper Zen understanding of the self as the ability to be present and grateful for what you have. Gilbert's pacing and style, her sentences and paragraphs, are virtually perfect.

Virginia Postrel, *The Future and Its Enemies*: As the editor of the libertarian magazine *Reason*, Postrel used her calm logic and good will to address issues that too often fall into the sludge of ideological and partisan strife. In this classic work, Postrel argues that the great conflicts of our time pit "dynamists" (those committed to exploration and human progress) against "stasists" (those who wish to preserve the status quo). Both dynamists and stasists can be found all along the ideological spectrum. A union organizer can be as much a stasist as the crabby retiree yelling at kids to get off his lawn; a detail-oriented banker can be as much a dynamist as a volunteer for the Bernie Sanders campaign. Postrel's crystal-clear writing and even-handedness make this wonky book a delight.